LEE Myung-Se

Korean Film Directors

The Korean Film Directors series is one of Korean Film Council's projects to furnish an international audience with insight and analysis into the works of Korea's most representative film directors.

The series aims to expand upon the existing body of knowledge on Korean film, educate the general public of the history of Korean film and Korean film directors, and draw attention to the significance of works that represent Korean film. Critics who share their insight in the series are leaders in their respective specialties. Each volume includes critical commentary on films, an extensive interview with the director, and a comprehensive filmography for reference.

LEE Myung-Se

Written by JANG Byung-won

Translated by KIM Min-hee

LEE Myung-Se

Written by JANG Byung-won

Korean Film Council
206-46 Cheongnyangni-dong, Dongdaemun-gu, Seoul 130-010, Korea
Phone (82-2) 9587-596
Fax (82-2) 9587-590
http://www.kofic.or.kr/english
email: sant0804@kofic.or.kr

Published by **Seoul Selection**
B1 Korean Publishers Association Bldg., 105-2 Sagan-dong, Jongno-gu, Seoul 110-190, Korea
Phone (82-2) 734-9567
Fax (82-2) 734-9562
http://www.seoulselection.com
email: pubco@seoulselection.com

ISBN: 978-89-91913-38-7 03680

Printed in the Republic of Korea

Contents

Preface	9
Introduction	15
On the Director	35
Interview	73
Biography	135
Synopsis	143
Filmography	159
About the Author	166
Index	167

Preface

Duelist, LEE Myung-Se's comeback film after a four-year stay in US, reflects his life as a film director. Similar to his previous film *Nowhere to Hide*, only set in a different time period during the Joseon Dynasty, the film conveys his enigmatic insights into movies through highly styled elements such as extremely minimalized narrative, abundant audio-visual images and a trademark mixture of reality, dream and fantasy, along with philosophical subjects such as 'chase' and 'confrontation.' As with his characters such as Detective WOO in *Nowhere to Hide*, obsessively chasing the cold-blooded criminal JANG Sung-min and Nam-soon of *Duelist*, who is after the 'Sad Eyes,' LEE's filmmaking for the last 20 years can be interpreted as 'chasing' itself. Starting from his rather impulsive decision to be a film director at the age of 17, he has been through a very tough journey to find the answer to his question 'What is film?' The quest continues to this day.

His directorial style has produced a filmography that is all about chasing the identity of film. His method of creating images is meditation. To visualize one significant scene in his film, he puts himself into a state of meditation. He often spends several nights, sometimes a whole month, to come up with one scene. This kind of filmmaking through 'inner pursuit' is possible because he is more of a freestyle artist than a formula-based one. LEE Myung-Se is not only well aware that film is different from any other preceding genre of art, but also devotes himself to make his vision a reality. His tendency to get to the bottom of it whatever the problem is can also be found in his style of filmmaking. This stubborn obsession often gets him the reputation of a 'fundamentalist.'

In an era when spiritual atmosphere in film art is increasingly on the wane, LEE Myung-Se is one of those rare artists eagerly searching for the real meaning of film. While the modern film industry does not care about this question as much as before, LEE continues his journey, chasing the answer for the essence of film. His films bear the fruits of his efforts to approach the expression and originality of films. LEE believes that those images caught within a camera frame are supposed to be elements of 'a small universe of film' different from the outer world. On the other hand, he continues to discipline himself to evolve beyond the limit of filmic expression. For inspiration, he looks to comics, paintings, music, poems, photography, fashion and even sports in order to get close to the essence of his cinematic concepts. With the belief that everything can be a method and source of creation, LEE intends to create 'integrated film' as a form of synthetic art. For this reason, his eight films show two seemingly different desires—a desire to explore the intrinsic characteristics of film and a desire to develop ways to expand the expressional techniques of film. These two contrary desires strangely coexist in his films.

LEE Myung-Se marks himself as a rare director in the history of Korean film. In the Korean film industry, where the tradition of realism is deeply rooted and influence from Western—especially Hollywood—movies prevails, it is rare to find a director so absorbed in pursuing the fundamental question, 'What is film?' Apart from a few directors digging into the subject these days, we can seldom find anyone who maintains this kind of attitude toward film. The reason for this is related to the time when LEE made his debut as a director. The late 1980s, when he began his career, was a period that witnessed many fundamental changes, not only in the

Korean film scene but also in society as a whole. Democratic movements were sweeping Korean society and the demand for democracy exploded everywhere. Korean film could not be free from this political upheaval. 'Freedom of expression' emerged as a critical issue and many films conveying the reality of Korean society and the political situation emerged to join the mainstream. Dubbed the 'Korean New Wave,' this trend was led by young directors such as PARK Kwang-su, JANG Sun-woo and PARK Jong-won, who turned sharp eyes on politics in an attempt to introduce a new format of film, defined as a 'realistic aesthetic,' which was conscious of the conflicting political situation with a critical viewpoint.

Although he started his career during this 'Korean New Wave' period, LEE didn't belong to the mainstream. His film had fundamentally different colors from the mainstream films of other directors. Even though he was one of the New Wave directors, he isolated himself by making films that were more about individual vision than radical political issues. Always pursuing new ways of communicating through films, LEE focuses more on the 'visual' of images and sound rather than the 'narratives' of huge themes or complicated storylines. The statement 'Make film with film' is central to him. LEE Myung-Se makes film telling stories only with images, adopting unconventional shot compositions, complicated camerawork, vivid colors, articulate drawings on screen and limited use of music. While other 'Korean New Wave' directors presented 'realism' in terms of aesthetics and tried to have a voice in a rapidly changing political situation with emphasis on storyline and subjects, LEE separated himself from this trend by establishing his own world of film with extremely individual vision, format and philosophy.

While making movies about love stories unattached to reality, the daily lives of the lower middle class, and imaginary fantasies based on his talents as a dreamer, LEE Myung-Se has elaborated his craftsmanship. Aspiring to be a craftsman rather than auteur, LEE can be called a sophisticated alchemist who can engrave images. His characteristic style, such as overlapping reality and dreams, artificially designing film sets like a stage play, and using cartoon-like images and unconventional music and sound shocked an industry dominated by conventional films. Unlike most 'New Wave' directors, who speculated more on storyline and style to talk about reality, LEE engrossed himself in finding out the identity of film as a cine-artist. If 'Korean New Wave' produced 'films of reflections' in line with a changing society, LEE Myung-Se can be said to have produced a real 'Cinema New Wave' pondering film itself, for the first time in Korean film history.

However, his films were categorized as exceptional and outstanding, and in the late 1980s when the Korean New Wave in the political sense began to prosper. Simply put, LEE Myung-Se had an international mindset. He didn't want to limit his films within the boundaries of Korea. Some critics vilified his films for being 'escapism lacking sociality' or 'aestheticism lacking a point.' Given the social situation, his film was destined to be blamed for being romantic and dreaming with excessive style.

If we remind ourselves, however, that too much realism has placed limits on the imagination in Korean films, LEE Myung-Se can be reevaluated as a lonely Don Quixote who has bravely tried to break though the limitations. In spite of being criticized for plots with unabashedly simple storylines and characters with childish mentalities, or being harshly judged for superficial subjects with poor stories, LEE hasn't compromised his filmmaking style for storyline or subject. He has never stopped chasing the 'fragrance' of film as an art, even in an era where it has disappeared. Even though audiences have often turned their faces away from his unusual style and critics haven't really welcomed the new style either, for this reason he has been able to keep introducing a radical film different from others.

As seen above, LEE's faith was based on his desire to take further steps into the core of filmic language. Since he made his first film, *Gagman*, he has been interested in finding ways to communicate solely through film itself, coming up with ones that no other directors had previously introduced. The characters in *Gagman* live between reality and dreams and do not give up their unrealistic dreams of becoming a director and actors. Their reckless attempt to escape from reality ends in failure, like any other daydream. Like a dream itself, the film shows LEE's thoughts about dreams and film .(According to LEE, he is often inspired by dreams to make films.) Believing that there's no reason or need to identify reality from dream or fantasy, he makes films as if dreaming and tries to convey that experience to the audience.

LEE Myung-Se is a 'rustic artist.' He identifies himself with artists who suffered dearly, including LEE Jung-seop, Vincent van Gogh and Charles-Pierre Baudelaire. He is a romanticist who believes that artists can find true meaning in life through their own tough lives. This comes from his own belief that art can be produced out of pain and extreme self-discipline, instead of compromising with a life of comfort. LEE leads a reclusive life, not even socializing with film people when he is not working on films. The only time he appears in the media is when his new movie needs publicity ahead of its release. The reason he can create unique films is because of this uncompromising 'inner search.' He has inscribed his own unique style on 100 years of Korean film history and evolved as an artist through the utmost endeavors in filmmaking. Despite working in the mainstream film industry, his attitude toward filmmaking and challenging spirit can be considered comparable to those of avant-garde experimental film artists.

I hope this book will be a guidebook to a 'movieist' director rarely found these days. There have been many people who have helped me in writing this book. I would like to give special thanks to Professor KANG Han-seop of the Film Department at the Seoul Institute of the Arts for allowing me to include his interesting personal stories about LEE Myung-Se as his friend and the director himself for sparing me a great deal of time in spite of his tight schedule during the post-production of his new film *M*.

Spring, 2008
JANG Byung-won

Introduction

This article was written by professor KANG Han-seop, the first film critic to acclaim LEE Myung-Se's film *Gagman* and an old friend of LEE for the last 20 years. Previously published in *FILM 2.0*, it has been included into this book with the permission of the author.

LEE Myung-Se and I

Without Rhyme or Reason

'I'm the very first director in the era of integrated film.' Those were the first words thrown at me, without rhyme or reason, by LEE Myung-Se, whom I both love and hate. It was at a plaza in front of Dansungsa Theater in Jongno-3-ga, Seoul, around 1 pm on June 24, 1989. The meeting was arranged at my request, on the day of the premiere of his first film *Gagman*. Earlier I had seen the film at an unofficial preview and it was a kind of shock to me.

I met him at the plaza where the audience stormed out of the theater after the first showing. He was dressed in a black shirt and trousers, and I complimented him on his film. It was at that very moment that LEE declared 'the era of integrated film' in such a determined tone and manner, as if he were a independence fighter of some sort, even before we were properly introduced.

That was 18 years ago. Since then he has become one of the leading directors in the Korean film circle, now enjoying almost the same level of prestige as master IM Kwon-taek does. I fire a question at this increasingly arrogant director.

'So, do you think you have made films that deserve the title 'the first director in the era of integrated film,' which you gave yourself more than a decade ago?' 'Sure! There has never been a single failure in my filmography, and I've been writing the generalities and particulars of integrated film theory while making each and every film of mine.' The dumbstruck critic asks the next question hopelessly. '(Sneeringly) Then who would be the second director in the era of integrated film?' 'Unfortunately, there's no one yet.' 'What? Then the integrated film you are talking about is nothing but the one-man religion that you created for yourself, isn't it? Didn't you once praise HONG Sangsoo and say that KIM Jee-woon had potential?' He looks embarrassed for a moment but immediately regains his composure, saying, as if it's a very pitiful thing. 'I don't see any new directors making their films from an evolutionary viewpoint. There is no single director who can see that a fish swims with a fin only because its legs degenerated. Most of them just focus on what the fish looks like externally.' I think to myself. 'Evolution? Degeneration? Legs? Fish? This hopeless fundamentalist is speaking nonsense. Has he already read my book, in which I declare myself the first critic of cultural evolutionary theory?'

What a director does as a creator and what a critic does as a reviewer are basically beyond human capability. Think about it. How can a human with imperfect sense and reason possibly analyze the infinity of a constantly changing world and universe and even judge whether it is good or bad? Creation and evaluation are not the domains of a human but of God, or it is just a timeless mystery one would never be able to understand. Long ago, when people knew their limits well enough to be humble, those who had special perceptive talents and wanted to play all day and keep asking questions either became shamans or secluded themselves for meditation on the provisions of nature.

However, those shamans are now well-respected as artists, and top-notch ones can ask for not only an enormous fee but also half of the production revenue. Also, argumentative whiz kids can make their living by giving lectures to mankind with every kind of pseudo-theory from all times and places. What a wonderful world! Creators and critics are ones who mistakenly believe that what is by nature impossible is a possible thing to do. These two occupations were created not by God but as part of a strategy for modern civilians to liberate themselves from autocratic power. Creators and critics are thus a kind of supermen who challenge the impossible, believing that they are the center of the world and that they can perceive, depict and criticize the world. They compete with the world with their pride and arrogance. They boast of being the best. Those who are after money and power are neither directors nor critics. LEE Myung-Se and KANG Han-seop know this very well, at the least. With this pride, we have fought each other for the last 18 years.

I'm Not the Kind of Director You Think I Am

LEE Myung-Se is a serious case of narcissistic personality. At school, he used to read novels in class, and during military service he had to go through a hard time as he was branded as 'the worst type of individualist.' I feel partly responsible for his narcissism, which seems now to be in the terminal stage. In 1989, celebrating the 70th anniversary of Korean film history, I chose *Gagman* as the best film of the year with the following comment: 'While BAE Yong-kyoon's *What is the Reason Bodhidharma Went to the East?* opened the door for the possibility of independent film in Korea, *Gagman* by LEE Myung-Se presented a new boundary for Korean film after 70 years of Chungmuro movies. The future of Korean film depends on the next 10 years, in which these two geniuses will play important roles.'

Gagman was scheduled to be released targeting the Christmas and New Year holidays in 1988. LEE Tae-won, the producer of this movie and the president of the Taeheung production company, was fascinated when it was screened for internal preview. But nobody else looked as enthusiastic about the film as he and LEE Myung-Se were. Besides, *Die Hard* had been released earlier and the

Hollywood blockbuster was breaking the records day by day as Christmas came near. With a lukewarm response from local distributors, the signboards for *Gagman* were finally removed. And the film only could be released with a minimal advertising campaign six months after its production was completed.

The failure was obviously predictable, considering the lack of any particular promotion and the indifferent responses of both the media and audience. It is the same now as in old times that a rookie director who has failed to earn either money or reputation would get prematurely expelled from the industry. Luckily for LEE Myung-Se, however, some people started a rumor about him saying that a new genius had appeared in Chungmuro. CHAI Yoon-hee, who currently leads the Committee of Women in Film Industry, was one of them. Back then, she was the director of Samho Film, a newborn production company with considerable financial resources, and her role in helping LEE make his second film was crucial.

One late afternoon on December 30, 1990, LEE Myung-Se and I were drinking a toast in a humble pub behind the Piccadilly Theater in downtown Seoul. We had just seen the standing signboard reading 'all tickets sold out' in front of the box office at the theater, which was showing his second film *My Bride, My Love*. After we played the 'making-a-bet-over-box-office-sales' game for a while, we returned to the confronting postures of director and critic.

'I enjoyed your film. I'm again convinced of your talent. In particular, the sequence in which Mi-young took a journey was very impressive, as it revealed your favorite theme, the relationship between reality and dreams, through the sincere and sharp observation of daily life.' After giving him this compliment out of courtesy, I began bombarding him with rather unfriendly questions. 'By the way, compared to *Gagman*, *My Bride, My Love* is no more than an étude.' 'I can't find any satire of anti-civilization and anti-system, full of pathos, which was found in *Gagman*. Compared to *Gagman*, this one is only superficial comedy.' 'Stylists of the worst kind like you tend to get trapped in anti-Enlightenment, searching for truth through self-reflection and ignoring the historic aspects of a changing world. Right then, the ghost of convention you hate will push your consciousness into the emptiness of individualization and conceptualization.' 'What makes LEE Myung-Se more like LEE Myung-Se is the destruction of the convention that fixes our thoughts and ideas, not the common realization we gain from ordinary life.' In spite of this shower of punches, he didn't seem to be bothered. After listening to all my malicious words, he wrapped up the conversation in just one line. 'You've got me wrong. I'm not the kind of director you think I am.'

LEE Myung-Se's Manager

One late night in mid-February, 1992, a small group of people were having drinks and talks in a motel room located in a small town in Gangwon Province. It was their first night of location hunting for LEE Myung-Se's third film, *First Love*. They were all quite excited, sensing the birth of a masterpiece, after reading the scenario. The group included Production Manager KIM Tae-kyun (director of *Volcano High School*), the production staff, myself, and the poet and director LEE Se-ryong, who later completed a brilliant anti-war script but had to give up the rights to it before the crank-up due to cerebral apoplexy.

We were busy infusing a great ambition into LEE, who had already become one of the best selling directors in Chungmuro. 'The script is absolutely fantastic.' 'It'll become a masterpiece.' 'No doubt a big box office hit.' I was acting like his biggest fan, forgetting that I was a professional critic who is supposed to be fair and objective. By the way, when we left the office on the morning of that day, we saw director KANG Woo-suk, who might have felt dejected after the failure of his film, *I Want to Live Just Until 20 Years Old*, staring at us with an envious look.

Unfortunately, while the season in the script was set as winter, the weather was already getting warmer, and the deep mountain snow was even beginning to melt. But LEE Myung-Se, in his 30s, was at the peak of his creativity. He immediately changed the season to spring. And he perfectly depicted everything about first love, a quivering experience that we all share, by combining and clashing images and sounds. I would definitely pick *First Love* as LEE Myung-Se's masterpiece among others. Or, rather, I would pick *First Love* as a national masterpiece among others.

'You created a masterpiece at the age of 35, which is a great achievement. But it's a pity that you have never reached that level again since.' Not surprisingly he didn't agree. 'Let me tell you again, there is no failure in any of my films. There are only changes made to accommodate the subject matter of each film. It is to get the essence out of it. The love in their last affair, the love of my bride and the first love are all equally important. Let me put it this way: My manager AHN Sung-ki, my Detective WOO, my Nam-soon and my Sad Eyes are all the best.' 'Don't be silly. Don't bluff. You found the secret of time at the age of 35. You gained it through your dreadful concentration, insight and intuition. You started from the thesis that 'First love does not evolve.' Of course, first love has been concealed, whether it's the 19th or 20th century. It is the same with young people in the 21st century. So first love is a clue to the secret of time, proving the eternal recurrence, just as the poet JEONG Hyun-Jong figured out and you showed perfectly in your films. In other words, you found the relativity of time. Now come on, confess. Admit that your sole masterpiece is *First Love*.' 'No, it's not. Like I said, there's no failure in my films whatsoever. Well, if you ask me my favorite, that would be *First Love*, *Nowhere to Hide*, and *Duelist*.' 'You're one stubborn fellow.'

On the morning of January 22, 1993, a group of people from LEE Myung-Se's fan club marched toward the Myungbo Theater. Waving their tickets in their hands, they greeted the director at the box office. There were almost 100 people, forming a long line in front of the theater. But that was it. The audience who had loved *My Bride, My Love* didn't show up. They turned a cold shoulder to it. *First Love* was condemned as kitsch, irrelevant to a Korean society going through rapid social and cultural transition. The box office sales for the first week were only 4,917! When I went to the Myungbo Theater to see him, LEE was standing alone at the entrance in a black trenchcoat. We went to a small Chinese restaurant nearby, ordered some alcohol and poured it down our throats. After talking about this and that, we ate some noodles to encourage ourselves and said our goodbyes. When I met him again after a long while, I asked him how frustrated he had felt on that day. He said to me, 'Actually, I felt grateful to God. I really did. Can you imagine how much more arrogant I would have been if my two films had been back-to-back big hits, considering I was already arrogant enough? I mumbled to myself, 'God! Thank you!' I really did.'

As the world began to dissent from LEE Myung-Se's film, I rose to save the genius. Whenever I was given a chance to judge at movie awards, I voted for LEE, his actors and his film crew. In 1993, the Blue Dragon Awards selected KIM Hye-soo in *First Love* as Best Actress. (The film perfectly reveals her purest beauty.) LEE was awarded the prize for best screenplay. This was natural, as he had expressed the theory of relativity through intuition. Other critics were dubious, but agreed with my advocacy of *First Love*. They did, however, turn down my suggestion to give the best film prize to *First Love*. The best film prize was given to *Sopyonje*, directed by IM Kwon-taek. The technical award went to *Blue in You*, with art direction by AHN Sang-soo. The resentment was relieved at the later Film Critic's Awards. The production design of *First Love*'s art director, CHO Young-sam, was the best that I had seen in Korean film. One day around that time, the critic KIM Jong-won introduced me at a meeting as 'LEE Myung-Se's manager.'

Crossing a Desert

In LEE's filmography, there were two periods of 'crossing a desert' through the decision of others, as a result of his films' box office failure, and two periods of 'voluntary rest' under the control of his own desire. The first 'desert' period was from January 1993, when *First Love* met with disaster at the box office, to the time when filming began on his next film *Affliction of Man*, and the second 'desert' period began in 1996, when *Their Last Love Affair* failed to get a good response from audiences, and lasted until early 1999.

During his first ordeal, I was unable to comfort LEE. At the time, I was ignorant and unruly. I forgot my mission as a scholar and mortgaged my soul to the KIM Young-sam government, a pathetic professor selling government-patronized sham film policy fitting in with today's argument for becoming 'one of the top five cultural powers,' for example saying that 'The profits of one *Jurassic*

Park is equal to the export value of 1.5 million Hyundai cars.' So I would start my day with breakfast, hold some lectures briefly in the morning, and then travel between various government committees, wasting my life building up minor wealth by appearing on the radio and television and accumulating worldly honors.

So I couldn't even go to the filming location for *Affliction of Man*. I might have missed the premiere, due to a somewhat busy schedule at that time, because I don't have any memory of it. Released in the middle of February 1995, *Affliction of Man* was a disaster both with audiences and critics. And then, one month after the release of the film, I received an emergency call from LEE Myung-Se asking for help. When we met in a cold studio apartment in Seocho-dong, LEE Myung-Se was shouting in exhaustion and disappointment. Losing his temper, he was cursing the ignorant critics and media in Korea. The consecutive failures of *First Love* and *Affliction of Man* troubled his peaceful mind.

He was as lonely and miserable as the unemployed manager AHN Sung-ki in the film. But he couldn't ride around on roller skates in the hallways or dance, splashing rainwater in the street. Instead, he analyzed every aspect of the failure in detail. He could even come up with a theory of a '20-year genre cycle' after investigating the statistics of box-office records. When I pointed out that he chose the wrong theme of layoffs and suicide in the year of 1995, which had been the most prosperous year in Korean history, he immediately struck back at my words. 'No way. Stories about poor people, miserable stories, always sell when life is good. Because they have the luxury. On the other hand, when life is not good, that luxury disappears and dramas with happy endings sell better.' Despite the fact that he was so good at making a strategy for successful films, his arrow missed the mark by a wide margin every time.

Thus, when he was fortunate enough to have the chance to make *Their Last Love Affair*, he could not escape his obsession with the idea that he would be permanently expelled from the film industry if he failed one more time at Chungmuro. So he took on the question, 'What is soft core pornography?,' through his own expert analysis. However, LEE's brand of soft core predictably failed when it premiered at Daehan Cinema, the largest theater in East Asia at that time. Critics turned their backs coldly. When I bumped into KANG Soo-yeon, star of the film, even she giggled, saying, 'You are the only critic who gave it 4 stars!' At the end of that year, I was appointed as the judge for pre-selection for the Daejong Award. Together with director PARK Jong-won, professor PYEON Jang-wan and the producer SHIN Chul, I managed to select *Their Last Love Affair* as a candidate film for 17 out of 18 Daejong Awards. And I went with LEE Myung-Se to Muju, Jeolla Province, where the main award ceremony was going to be held. As a result, the film set a new record as the film nominated for the most awards without winning. The year's star at the Daejong Awards was CHANG Yoon-hyun, director of *The Contact*. We shared a car with CHANG on the way back to Seoul. At one small café we stopped by on the way back, CHANG mentioned, 'Young directors in our generation keep studying LEE Myung-Se's *First Love* over and over.' A very smart and wise man, that CHANG...

LEE Myung-Se spent a very lonely period from the summer of 1996 to the end of 1998, so we often met each other. LEE Myung-Se, the erstwhile dictator of the film set, was busy attending premieres with a critic. He also gave lectures at a few colleges, despite not having so many students ready to welcome an unsuccessful film director. He could even spare extra time to have drinks with the students in my class on our college's freshmen orientation trip. Then, one day, something happened. Richard Corliss, a critic from TIME magazine, introduced *Their Last Love Affair* as a fascinating example of Korean film, devoting a considerable section in his article on the Toronto Film Festival to this subject. I excitedly told him on the phone that he was in TIME, and with a photo to boot. Copying and translating the original article into Korean, I distributed the copies to reporters at a premiere. Several newspapers ran articles saying how 'TIME gave high praise to LEE Myung-Se.' It is an episode that shows our immaturity at that time.

Craftsman

I often worry that LEE Myung-Se might be found dead at a film studio during post-production the next time he makes a film. He is such a perfectionist that he would risk his life for filmmaking. Whenever he finishes one film, he ages at least 10 years. As a result, he looks a lot older than I do, even though we are of a similar age. His commitment to craftsmanship can be found in a line spoken by Detective WOO (PARK Joong-hoon) in the 1999 film *Nowhere to Hide*, the last film of the last century: 'Judgment is to be made by a judge, a defense is to be made by a lawyer, forgiveness is the part of the pastor, and a detective should only care about catching criminals.'

Nowhere to Hide was the only film of LEE's for which I didn't write a review. At that time, I lost interest in reviews and started to meet with producers and investors to discuss scenarios, as I wanted to produce LEE Myung-Se's film. All those people found the plan interesting, but didn't accept LEE Myung-Se as a director. They couldn't accept a director known for corny dramas directing an action film, with an urban setting at that. Even the producer SHIN Chul, who has always admired LEE Myung-Se, said, 'Han-seop, the scenario itself is very good,' but couldn't come up with anything after that. LEE also had numerous meetings with producers. For a while we believed East Film, run by the famous actor MYUNG Kae-nam, might take the plan. But one day LEE Myung-Se called me up and said in a very rattled voice: 'You know what, LEE Chang-dong told me the script shouldn't be written like this.' The script was passed around Chungmuro once again and eventually was taken by Taewon Entertainment. The film became hugely successful and LEE Myung-Se regained his reputation. And then the 21st century began. However, LEE Myung-Se couldn't cope with production companies. Sick of the production system at Chungmuro, he decided to reform the field of Korean film.

Brooklyn and E-mail

In the summer of 1999, when LEE met with great success with *Nowhere to Hide*, I expected to receive about two million won, including the interest for the original amount of one million won he borrowed from me a few years ago. However, it was my fault that I didn't document the debt, relying on my trust in him. Having shaken off numerous proposals for a follow-up film project from producers, one night in the winter of that year, when we were drinking with each other, he stated, 'There's nothing more to achieve in our country,' a statement as trembling as his girlish visual style, and then declared, 'I will move to Hollywood and come back after I've won against the best film directors in the world.' As I was dejected at the prospect of not being paid back the money I had loaned him, he told me in a serious tone, 'I will pay you back at compound interest in dollars.'

The following April, he boarded a plane bound for New York, flying over the Pacific Ocean. He was savvy enough to keep in touch with his contacts by phone and e-mail. He even came back several times to make sure the supporters who might forget him would keep him in mind, saying that he had completed an incredible horror film without a drop of blood and received a positive response from Ridley Scott's production team.

However, the apex of his time in Brooklyn had nothing to do with Ridley Scott, the Sundance Film Festival, or the European Retrospective Film Festival. He expanded his horizons and deepened his thinking on films by watching and studying so many classic films in New York. And finally, he literally became a film philosopher. Among the e-mails he sent to people in Korea, one sent on October 2, 2001 is a highlight.

> 'I'm still trembling with excitement, and still speechless. It's because I finally found someone I can finally confess my love to. He already knew the words I was meaning to say and had the feelings I was trying to express. I could finally clear my thoughts, which might have remained buried for so long if I hadn't found him. The encounter happened at two o'clock today—more precisely, two o'clock, October 1st. The gloomy weather (it has been like this for the last few days) and rain almost kept me from going out. What if I hadn't gone? It would have happened later anyway, if there's any karma, but it would have taken longer.

Strangely, I got up early this morning, which is not normal, since I usually like to stay in bed as long as possible. I even felt good enough to go out early to be there with 30 minutes to spare. I was just waiting with a cup of coffee. I took my seat five minutes before the session. Although this place is usually full of young people, today there were more older viewers than young ones, since it was still daylight. At exactly two o'clock, a pianist started to play and the lights went off. And then he appeared, amid applause and laughter.

His name is Buster Keaton. Today he presented us with the story of The CameraMen (1949). I once mentioned to you that there are 5 directors who made film with film: Ozu Yasujiro, Federico Fellini, Charlie Chaplin, Jacques Tati and Buster Keaton. I made a list of them after I came here. It occurred to me when I happened to rent Roma from the library early this year that I would love to make a list of the directors who made film with film. At that time there was a retrospective of Jacques Tati's films, with Les Vacances de Monsieur Hulot and I included him on the list thinking that was a film with film. After watching a video of the film Steamboat Bill Jr. by Buster Keaton, whom people often mentioned whenever I picked Chaplin as my favorite director, I decided to put his name on the list.

Today I became really convinced that he is the one who makes film with film. He was saying exactly what I was thinking. He knows what kind of story has to be chosen for a film. He understands about the space required. We usually think that everything can be expressed in film. But this is not true, because film can express only the cinematic. This is definitely the limit for film. Just as a human's life has a time limit, we have to admit the limits of film. The limitation could be the original characteristic for any kind of art.

He says that film should stay simple, simple meaning quintessential. Therefore a good film cannot be an object of analysis, because essence cannot be further split. Essence is for further interpretation, not for analysis. This is like implicit questions and answers. For example, how would you analyze the exact meaning of 'Why don't you have tea before you leave?' In conclusion, 'something to be analyzed is not yet quintessential.' Additionally, it could be said, as Franz Kafka commented, that a poem cannot be a religion, but it can be a prayer. In spite of more stories I would like to tell you, but I'm still too excited. When I walked out, I made a confession of my love for Buster Keaton. This is the first time I'm telling you my confession.

LEE Myung-Se

P.S. Han-seop, are you doing well?

At first I felt really good after reading his e-mail. I could bear the deferred payment if he was studying this hard. On the other hand, his words that 'a good film should not be analyzed' might have been intended to disarm film critics like me who make a living by tearing apart, dividing and disassembling films. But I could understand him. When I showed his mail to some students, some looked quite touched and somehow teary-eyed. However, I'm not that sentimental a writer. So I warned the students who were about to turn fetishistic toward his e-mail: 'LEE Myung-Se is the equivalent of Osama Bin Laden in film philosophy. Watch out!' Here are my thoughts.

'I know the five men who make film with film,' 'Only the cinematic can be expressed by a film,' and, 'Film has to be kept simple. Being simple is the same as being quintessential.' These claims by LEE Myung-Se are based on the discourse from medieval epistemology pursuing transcendent truth as everlasting essence, which can be reached by disciplining mind and body. It is clearly wrong that all things and phenomena have an eternal essence and that it can be recognized through souls. Even before we refer to modern philosophers, we simply don't have an organ called a soul in the human head.

This is why I believe that there's no true way for film art. In other words, the essence of film continuously changes. Whereas the film itself does not contain any meaning, the meanings can be created from the combination and relations between the creator, film and audience and the circumstances where they stand relative to each other. Moreover, fundamentalists are always dangerous. Since they suppose that the truth can exist solely by itself, they do not admit what others believe.

Muslim fundamentalists like Bin Laden and imperialists seeking hegemony like George W. Bush are all harmful beings with regard to world peace.

The only difference with artistic fundamentalists like LEE Myung-Se or Andrei Tarkovsky is that they can sublimate their rage toward the philistine world into beauty. Thus, even though they misunderstand the foundations of film, they leverage the misunderstanding to go down the well of film art deeper to reach the stratigraphic abyss, to touch the boiling magma.

World Created by the Convicted

Three of the greatest late film directors enshrined into God's great Pantheon came to see LEE Myung-Se. Chronologically, they are Orson Welles, Alfred Hitchcock, and Ozu Yasujiro. He bumped into Orson Welles at a zoo. A chubby gentleman was walking ahead of him and turned to look at LEE Myung-Se for a while. Speculating on the meaning of this, LEE cast director BAE Chang-ho in his film *Gagman*. Is a film a dream or nostalgia, or a dream within a dream? Ozu, a kind man, was writing something at LEE's desk. This happened when LEE was working on *Nowhere to Hide*. Pleased to see him, LEE greeted him and went out of the room to serve him tea, but found him gone when he came back. What would be the common code between Ozu's *I Was Born, But...* and LEE's *Nowhere to Hide*? On his encounter with Hitchcock, LEE confessed the following in an e-mail he sent in March 2002:

> 'Without the news of cherry blossoms in Tongyeong that I heard from a friend, I would have confused this spring season with an unusual weather phenomenon. I can feel that it's spring, especially when I open my window without feeling cold. How are you doing? You must be busy with the same old new semester at school. I'm pleased to tell you that the second script is currently going well. I also finally realized what my dream of 10 years ago meant. I have been thinking about the meaning of when Hitchcock showed me the letter M in my dream. It could mean

'misty,' 'mystery' or 'murder'... so I've added the misty background in my films since then. The misty scene in *First Love* is linked with the dream. But I realized it was just like a finger pointing up at the moon. M stood for MacGuffin. So I can tell you what my next film will show you. It is a commercial film entitled *MacGuffin*.'

And then in 2004, LEE Myung-Se packed up and left New York and returned to Seoul, establishing Production M at the Namsan campus of the Seoul Institute of the Arts, to film *Duelist*, which he labeled 'the most brilliant sensory action film in history.' So what is the 'M' this time? Is it the MacGuffin, the artificial device of excitement, fear and passion that draws the audience into the film? When I threw this question to students in my class during a 'script workshop' for the purpose of 'finding a successful script X,' there were a few interesting answers that they came up with. 'M is a shadow. Larger than actual size and it disappears when you look back.' 'M stands for a muffin at McDonald's. The muffin is yummy but Dunkin Donuts are more delicious.' They sometimes teach me rather than learn from me. They're my teachers.

LEE's updated answer is that 'M stands for every word starting with it. Misty, mystery, murder, Marilyn Monroe, M school...' Attacking his strange theory, I mentioned, 'These days, M must mean money for you.' Then director KIM Hong-joon, sitting next to me, helped out by saying 'Could be 'more money.' It definitely goes past 'more money' into 'maximum money.'

Boasting at the Center of the World

Now back to the beginning. Let's take a look at what integrated film is and whether LEE Myung-Se is really a director second to none. First of all, the idea about integrated film is great itself. However, if we expect too much, disappointment is inevitable. That's because the words are great, but at the same time obvious.

'Integrated film destroys the boundary between drama and documentary. Dividing image and sound is mainly for some European art film director who tends to divide the physical and mental aspects, even when the art and money have one purpose and the confrontation between the message and the visuals is not necessary. The genre theory based on '4 minds and 7 emotions' could be useful only for a production line-up in a major Hollywood production. There are two reasons. First, the world can't be divided into two. Secondly, when an artist experiences a spiritual enlightenment, realizing that world is indivisible, he or she will have the insight to express the same substance beyond difference or division, able to describe the beginning and end as the same.

'And that's right. It's reasonable. It's proper. However, the reason for being for an artist is to long for the world where everything was united, not yet segmented. And it's the work of the scientist to risk everything to sever and divide things in search for the most fundamental substance of the world. Since essence as the minimum and basic and expression as the maximum and phenomenon are linked to each other, both the artist and scientist have to go back and forth from one side to the other, between the opposites. The only difference is that scientists count on numbers and formulas while artists rely on image and metaphor to explain and express the world. Didn't you know that? LEE Myung-Se, you are truly audacious to pursue the essence of the world, but you are not the only one. There are many directors in pursuit of same thing, such as JANG Sun-woo and KIM Ki-duk...And if you go out into the rest of the world, there are too many courageous directors to count.'

However, he didn't even pretend to listen to this excellent explanation from the number one critic in cultural evolutionary theory. And then he explained that the main faculty members in his M school are those five individuals—Ozu, Fellini, Tati, Chaplin and Keaton—and that he is the number one director attempting to integrate the worlds of these five men.

The rcsponse to the film *Duelist* consisted of 30% enthusiasm, 30% glibness, 30% dissatisfaction and the rest disinterest. 'Why didn't you add at least one dramatic kissing scene between GANG Dong-won and HA Ji-won, if you were hoping for the film to be a blockbuster?' I asked him, and his impudent answer was that the sound of the blades colliding in the duel scene makes something like a 'smooch smooch' kissing sound. Dumbstruck, I pointed out other things: 'The script is full of problems. The first is the absence of the two most important plot points. The first question is why Sad Eyes and Nam-soon fall in love with each other and the other is why Sad Eyes betrays Byung-jo, the Chief Minister.' And he answered back, 'Film is poetry and image, not a novel,' and referred to the 'mot juste' theory of Gustave Flaubert, seemingly testing my qualifications as a professor.

I can't say anything to him, though I too currently fight against snobbish film theories with all my mighty will. He is already self-centered and full of confidence. When a reporter challenged him with the comment, 'You are like a child who is not yet mature,' he simply answered, 'Film is something that is young forever.' When I decided to leave, having run out of interest with this roundabout conversation, I declared to him, 'Boasting at the center of the world, that's what survival is.' And then again, this self-righteous LEE Myung-Se said that no, film is not about boasting, it is sending out love letters, even slips of paper to audiences. And like a letter of good fortune, it can spread around the world, one after another like dominos. He says that the viewer is a fisherman. They are supposed to catch as many fish as possible among the countless ones released by the number one director of integrated film. LEE's films now need to succeed commercially. So LEE Myung-Se must go a bit astray. Otherwise he will be calling me up again to have drinks until the break of dawn, raving about true film, the essence of film, etc., etc.

Written by KANG Han-sup,
a professor of the Film Department, Seoul Institute of the Arts

On the Director

THE FIU SEVENTEENTH
MIAMI FILM FESTIVAL

LEE Myung-Se, a Master of Integrated Film, or Homo-cinemacus

'Precisely 10 years ago, I had a dream one night. In that dream, someone showed me the character M. And it became a lifelong question to me. What on earth does M stand for? M, misty, mystery, movie, money, *metiere*, Myung-Se... Probably after that, my films have always had misty scenes. The foggy scene in *First Love* was the start. Time flows, and I sometimes forget about the question. Although a Zen master once told me that a monk in meditation should utter 'Oh, my topic!' instead of 'Ouch!' even when he tumbles over, I'm forgetful of the topic sometimes. And time passes by.

As it may be with anyone in the film business, I always think about what film is. And I develop the question a bit further—What is commercial film? Or sometimes, what is the public? What is the audience? And back to 'what is film?' again, and mix all the questions. One day, exactly 10 years after I started to have these questions, I realized that M stands for MacGuffin. M could be Myung-Se, *metiere*, money, misty, mystery, media, metro, mass communication and so forth. But, simply put, it is MacGuffin.

Everything turns out to be a MacGuffin, including the Bible, the Sutras and life. Everything is like a finger that points at the moon, not the moon itself. The finger is important because it's pointing at the moon. Thus, the Bible is important, the Sutras are important and life is important. Love is a MacGuffin, too. That's why a Zen master said, 'If you meet Buddha, kill Buddha, if you meet a mentor, kill the mentor and if you meet parents, kill the parents.' Because everything is a MacGuffin. Yeah, that's right. Kill everything. If you meet a film, kill the film, and this is what the MacGuffin is all about. Maybe the MacGuffin is just one matchstick, worth less than a penny, but it can light up the darkness to find a hidden pearl. A MacGuffin is no substance itself, but exposes substance. That's why a storyline in commercial film is always important as a MacGuffin.

The eyepatch the pharmacist is wearing in *My Bride, My Love* is also a MacGuffin. PARK Joong-hoon's walking style is also a MacGuffin. What on earth is the MacGuffin? It's a dream. It's Zhuangzi's dream. Did he dream the butterfly's dream? Or did the butterfly dream his dream? Which one is true? Go find out.'

- Extracts from an article by LEE Myung-Se,
sent to the film magazine *Kino* from New York, 2002

LEE Myung-Se's eighth film *M* is about the novelist Min-woo, who tracks down his lost memory of first love. His journey following the trace of the first love represents LEE's own resolution not to lose his first memory and first mind toward filmmaking. The film, with dazzling audio-visual images, unconventional style and a mystery plot to reveal the secret of 'M,' seems like LEE's declaration of will to recover the passion for life and inspiration of art. As shown above in his writing for a film magazine, 'M' is the topic he has been struggling with for the last 10 years.

LEE Myung-Se is a craftsman as well as a reformist who has been infusing the

M, 2007

atmosphere of innovation into the Korean film industry. Since the idea of becoming a director struck him on the street at 17, he has been persistently chasing the question, 'What is film?' Although it has been almost 30 years since he started his career, LEE is still burning with the passion for film art and exhausts all his energy making each film. His almost religious faith in film and purism on art are absolutely exceptional. Being an iconoclast, LEE has maintained his style of filmmaking, constantly questioning the limitations of the conventional realist aesthetics from which Korean film has been having a hard time escaping. And, as a result, he has broadened the horizon of Korean film aesthetics to some extent. The films that are the fruits of his labors prove that the cinematic language is a continuously evolving organism instead of an unchangeable system. LEE Myung-Se's self-assigned life mission is to create a new film containing what he thinks is the essence of film, while denying the common notions of the existing filmic grammar. So, what he needed more than anything else from the moment he decided to be a film director was a film theory based on his own philosophy. His idea of film was developed from the general concept shared by all fields of art.

LEE's reputation has been built on his rollercoaster career of cyclical success and failure. For the past 20 years, he has made films neither to appeal to the public's tastes nor to enlighten the general public's consciousness or depict the misery of reality. When he made his debut at the end of 1980s, LEE was categorized as neither 'socialist' nor left-wing, which was prevailing in the Korean film circle at the time. The approach to image was different from other directors. Since he educated himself, his thoughts on film did not develop through learning or training under the established education system. That was rather fortunate for him. The education that Korean film establishment could offer at the time was trapped in dogma. It was just cramming and repeating obsolete theories that failed to reflect the dynamic changes of modern films. Filled with pure passion and enthusiastic curiosity, LEE has devoted himself to finding the essence of film. While reviving the disappearing tradition of film, he has been trying to trace the evolution of the film image entering upon a new phase.

Descriptions like 'obstinate dictator' or 'awful director who doesn't know how to compromise' are tagged to LEE Myung-Se. Since he started his career as a production staff member, LEE was criticized for being a Hitler, and had to suffer vicious rumors each time he made films. Normally he is a nice guy, but when it comes to filmmaking, he is one hell of a hard-liner who knows no compromise. It was the same when he went to New York to prepare for his next film. He aspired to cross national borders and advance to the center of international film industry, but LEE was never going to give up his privilege of absolute freedom as a creator for it. No different from 20 years ago, he makes films sticking to his own style and ideas, with the stubbornness which can only be found in an artist who never cares about what's going on around the world.

As the result of his struggle with the same old question, 'What is film?,' LEE has established the 'integrated film theory,' which puts in order not only all the genres of art but also every aspect of life, philosophy and aesthetics. He tries to integrate the characteristics of adjacent media such as painting, photography and literature, and develop the cinematic language at the same time. These two contrary desires are the true colors of LEE's cinematography. The quest for the essence and evolution of film is where LEE Myung-Se's lifelong search begins.

Treason Against Realism and Reestablishment

The 30 years of LEE Myung-Se's life as a film director have seen a lot of ups and downs. While he made some big hit films like *My Bride, My Love* or *Nowhere to Hide*, he also made 'cursed' movies that disappeared amid a cold reception from audiences, such as *First Love*. Sticking to his own world with extreme obstinacy, LEE has been pursuing the meaning of 'being cinematic.' But some present the criticism that his narcissistic world of cinema is degrading. Even when the films he made with the utmost efforts flop at the box office and get hammered by critics, LEE doesn't get dejected, but encourages himself with a fighting spirit, claiming that he is a rookie who prepares for the future of film, which, he sees, is still in the quickening period. It is quite strange that, although LEE raises a lot of various issues in his films, there are rarely proper reviews focusing on these issues as much. It is partly because the opinions of him always go bipolar, but the main reason should be that his films are not easy to analyze or explain in the first place.

It was in 1989 that LEE Myung-Se's first movie came out to the world. Released one year after completion following some twists and turns, *Gagman* was one of the most controversial debut films produced in the 1980s. The film was LEE's daring declaration toward film, portraying the escape story of a third-class gagman chirping like a lark. *Gagman* was the compilation of his thoughts that had accumulated for 10 years while he was apprenticing in film production. The film revolves around film. *Gagman*, which seems like a love letter to the era of romantic films, was based on personal experience. By putting his thoughts into the voice of LEE Jong-se in the film, saying, 'The era of the masterpiece is gone,' the director summarizes his thoughts on film, which accumulated for 10 years in Chungmuro.

Gagman, 1988

Many autobiographical elements can be found in *Gagman*, the storyline of which is said to have been written just in one day.

His thoughts and various viewpoints on film, along with his influences, appear here and there in the film. However, no proper review was written about it. It was because *Gagman* was pointing to a spot where Korean films had never explored up until then.

LEE's films are often considered heretical, and this may have something to do with Korean film's orientation toward realism. The realist aesthetic that had been dominant in Korea until the early 90s brought with it the obsession that film, too, should directly reflect the social reality. On the other hand, 'the principle of verisimilitude,' which is the framework of Hollywood dramas, dominated the Korean film scene. LEE tried to overcome the exclusivity of Korean film aesthetics.

He tried to convince people that film is more than reality and that only what can be experienced through film is 'truth.' *Gagman*, which was inspired by Don Quixote and Sancho Panza from the novel by Cervantes, shocked the Korean film world at the time, in which realism was followed as the absolute value. *Gagman* was a controversial film denying the realist assumptions prevailing in Korean films. LEE insists that absolute rules of realism should be doubted. In his idea of realism, reality includes thinking, dream and fantasy, which feel perfectly real to us when we experience them. A direct example is shown in the scene where AHN Sung-ki gives a monologue on his past on the beach.

Korean films, based on social realism in their subject matter and Hollywood's classical realism in their form, have faithfully abided by the watchword of realism that film should reflect or restore reality and depict the seemingly probable reality in a plausible way. However, LEE denies both 'the aesthetics of verisimilitude' that values only sensible stories and 'the reflection theory' that film, rooted in real life, should be the reflection of reality. His films explicitly show silly daydreams, simple love stories, self-consciousness, excessive style and the absence of historical perspective. LEE was a foreigner in the realism-oriented world. Those who found something fresh and new in his films were enthusiastic about his liberal ideas and imagination, unattached to conventional realism, and on the other hand, those who branded him a senseless art supremacist denounced him for denying the realism thesis.

In that sense, LEE Myung-Se was like an unidentified flying object. *Gagman* ends with an announcement that everything was a dream. In the film, dream and real life, past and present, fantasy and reality are mingled all together with no particular boundaries. The same is true of *First Love*. The film follows the creation, progress and extinction of a feeling of love by showing the status of imagination and feeling, rather than the development of dramatic events. His films disapprove of differentiating and drawing borders and deny all the fixed frameworks making boundaries. The domain of realism he seeks is not limited to what can be seen or recorded. It includes thinking, dream and fantasy and he also thinks what can be called 'unreal' or 'imaginary' could be regarded as reality if it feels real. He believes that the differences between real and unreal, between reality and fantasy, between past and present, between existence and non-existence and between visible and invisible, are all created by humans. LEE's aversion to boundaries is revealed in a style of camerawork that links the inside and outside of a frame.

In his recent films, this trend has been reinforced, as found especially in chaotic scenes that cause extreme confusion. Such a concept is visualized in several scenes in *M*. The camera movement draws links between the inside and outside of the frame. The moving lines of characters in alleys and Min-woo's apartment and the camera movement proceed in the way that removes the division of inside and outside. As the characters wander in alleys or walk up and down the apartment, the space is not perceived coherently. The inside becomes the outside and the outside becomes the inside. It's all the same labyrinth. While the film crosses between the past and present, between dream and memory, the distinction between the two is not clear. LEE Myung-Se seems to believe that such distinction is neither easy nor necessary to make. That is exactly what *M* makes us feel puzzled when we watch it. Nothing is clear. Dream and real life, past and present, reality and fantasy are mixed with each other. The 'reflection' frequently used in *M* is the concept to show this. In the film, mirrors, reflective glass and see-through glass appear, without fail, in Min-woo's apartment, on the streets and alleys. These are set to use the small space more efficiently for filming, but also to erase the borders. It's the same for the photo hanging on the wall in the seafood restaurant. The endless repetition of rooms in the photo appears to be embracing both the inside and the outside. This world view of LEE Myung-Se denies the old principle of realism that only visible things can be called real. His films prove that realism can be created without any direct correspondence to reality.

Dream and Memory, a Form of Cinematic Time

LEE Myung-Se's keywords to overcome the dogma of conventional realism aesthetics are dream and memory. The characters created in his films are all dreaming or living in a dream. LEE puts dream scenes in almost every film. Dreams are the ground for unreality. The colorfully decorated offices or houses that often appear in his films don't seem to hide the fact that they are film sets. The seemingly out-of-reality settings are aimed to dull the sense of reality. The reason why LEE frequently uses memory, dream and fantasy is not because he has nostalgia for the past but because he believes that the past keeps influencing our life and spirit of the present. LEE thinks that dream makes possible an intense cinematic experience which cannot be gained in real world.

The reason why LEE volatilizes the sense of reality is because he does not approve the boundary between dreams and reality. Such disapproval of 'drawing a boundary line' is another characteristic of his films. From his debut film *Gagman* to his most recent film *M*, LEE has often shown dreamer characters who freely come and go between dreams and reality. Dream is a part of life, not a story. The dreams or daydreams of the characters in his film remind us of things we already know but we don't like to remember. It is not that dreams or imagination is all unreal or false. The thoughts and feelings of characters are just expressed through their dreams or imagination. Dreams are neither imagination nor unreality. Although we always dream a dream and remember it vividly in our daily life, we also have the prejudiced view that a dream is always unreal and absurd. To LEE Myung-Se, however, a dream is a tangible reality and something substantial that stays close with us all the time.

The fact that LEE's film is full of unreal images has something to do with this attitude toward dreams and imagination. Memories and remembrances are already in the domain of the past, but still it's a sad thing to let them go. A dream is like a voice calling back things that disappeared or were forgotten. This is the reason why LEE constantly throws the essential question of 'What is film?' or why the memories of first love make frequent appearances in his films. His tendency to return to dreams, memory and the first moment is often criticized as a 'regression.' It is in the same context that his films are often blamed as a plethora of unsubstantial images or rootless films without genealogy. This lack of understanding is due to the different approach to the image. Perfectly controlling the situation to get the scene he wants, LEE is a master of creating the space of dream and imagination.

Let's take a look at several fantasy scenes for an example. LEE Jong-se in *Gagman* says the following to himself: 'Is everything we see only a dream in a dream, or does it seems to be?' The film ends with the answer, showing that the series of robberies his gang committed were all a dream. It's the same when sleepwalking manager AHN Sung-ki in *Affliction of Man* becomes involved in a night concert playing together with neighborhood beggars. In another scene in the film, he is floating in an office full of soap bubbles. Both scenes are dreamlike and imaginary, but they visualize what's inside the character's consciousness. Jumping any moment from reality into unreality or the imaginary world and showing the truth of 'invisible' consciousness—this is LEE's filmic style. To him, what is happening in one's consciousness, or whether it is 'cinematic truth' or not, is far more important than whether it is a reality or a dream. *First Love* is filled with fantasy scenes as well. When Young-shin rides a bicycle to meet her beloved Chang-wook, the bicycle floats in the air as if it is flying. This depicts her emotional state rather than reality. The flying bicycle visualizes Young-shin's fluttering heart and happiness. In the same way, the bicycle in front of Chang-wook's house moves by itself, and an empty cup fills with coffee and the cup floats in Chang-wook's room.

Through memory, dream and fantasy, we can witness what we imagine in our mind taking place in reality. The memory and the dream are based on general human experiences, not on abstract notions. The memories LEE Myung-Se revives are not the debris of grandiose metaphysics or hackneyed thoughts, but of an extremely primitive and universal nature. For example, they are like the objects appearing at the beginning of *First Love*. The objects, like a notebook, an ink bottle, a coffee cup, a bicycle, an umbrella, a kettle, an old camera, a mailbox, an old radio and letters, are to be seen later in the film and bring nostalgia to us. And they are inscribed with the traces of time. Things of reminiscence, such as a small neighborhood comic book shop, a barbershop, a charcoal briquette shop, an old phonograph, a bicycle with a headlight and an old photo album, create the feeling

First Love, 1993

and time that correspond to what LEE wants to express in his films. The space and objects evoking feelings of nostalgia have the traces of time. Like a 'souvenir in our minds,' an alley with small shops huddled together, a railroad and a movie theater rekindle memories for all of us. Giving life to such space and objects, LEE Myung-Se presents 'imaginary reality' rather than the 'reenacted reality' that realism highly values.

Dreams and memory are aroused by 'sense.' Places in memory are very real, but imagining them is not real. So some devices are used as a reminder. In *M*, the scenes in Min-woo's dream are real moments that existed in the past and still exist with tangible objects (such as Mi-mi's hair and a matchbox from the Lupin bar). In his dream appear the beauty salon where his first love was 11 years ago, dazzling sunshine, the noisy sound of singing cicadas, a song he used to sing shyly, a romantic bicycle trip, movies they watched together, the scent of a cheap soap, the rain linked to Mi-mi's death and an umbrella. Things he remembers one after another help him in his time travel. His presence is swallowed by a pitch-black darkness, but the past in his memory shines brilliantly. When our past and memory are overlapped with cold reality, we realize what was lost and forgotten. The past was not terminated, but prolongs to the present. The effort to revive memory that was thought to have disappeared is different from retrograde nostalgia. The first love in both *First Love* and *M* and the inspiration it brings are all felt as real. Time is not cut off but dissolved. The past does not disappear but overlaps. The same goes for the memory of first love.

The reason why LEE Myung-Se is attached to dream and memory is because they present 'cinematic time.' LEE's idea of dream and imagination is clearly revealed in *First Love* and *M*, which is a sort of sequel to *First Love*. *M* can be said to show the story after *First Love*. The concept of time can be drawn from here. Time keeps flowing in the objects or space in the camera. There are traces of a number of people and many memories being inscribed, and time continues.

The changes in the alley, where Min-woo and Mi-mi's love blossomed and where a beauty salon and a laundry shop were located, show the 'time' of 11 years. In *First Love*, Young-shin loses her love, but time passes by. In the alley in front of her house, autumn leaves fall, snow comes and flowers blossom the following spring. After people leave, a new shop opens and the street looks different, but the traces remain somewhere. The last scene of *My Bride, My Love* also shows Young-min, after time passes, having become a father. In *M*, Min-woo dimly recalls those times when he grabbed the door handle of the Lupin Bar and when he first held Mi-mi's hand in front of the Mona Lisa hair shop at the end of their date. In the past, Min-woo could meet Mi-mi in the hair shop, but now he can meet Mi-mi's ghost only in the Lupin. The song 'Fog,' which links the past to the present, is the song that his father sang to himself whenever he drank, the song Min-woo taught to Mi-mi and the song that awakens Min-woo's memories at the Lupin.

Like this, 'memory' is the act of being aware of time. As an act of realizing the flow of time and getting close to secrets, memory is a significant element in LEE's film. LEE Myung-Se seeks to open the door of time and search for faint memories and the original image of dreams. Although a terrible reality comes from the lost first love and lapse of memory, he considers the value of things lost by retracing time. This could be interpreted as LEE's actual plaintive wish to recover the first memory of 'film.' Chasing after first love is his attitude toward film, as well as his resolution to start over again from the first moment when he decided to become a director. Despite 30 years of time blunting his early passion, he attempts to go back to the passion of the old days, like Min-woo recovering his withered inspiration in *M*.

From the small objects and spaces preserved in the storage of memory, LEE designs his method of rumination and recollection. The devices revealing this most clearly are the mirror and window. His camera frequently moves inside through the window or observes inside from outside. For instance, in the film *First Love*, the image of Young-shin observing the first encounter of Chang-wook, who has come as a guest teacher to the theatrical play class, and his friends are observed by the camera from outside. In the film *My Bride, My Love*, the camera seems to spy into the honeymooning couple's house as it moves stealthily over the window frame. There is also Mi-mi staring at Min-woo playing the guitar through the window in the classroom in *M*. The 'window' is a device to peep into memory as well as a metaphor for the screen. As we watch the film through the screen, we also look at stories through the window.

Searching for Concept, Not Technique

LEE Myung-Se has received divided reviews so far. There is no 'middle ground' in attitudes toward his films. Enough for someone to comment that the world can be divided into those who love LEE's films and those who hate them, LEE stands between extremely different points of view. Whether one is hostile or favorable to him, he is most often labeled a 'stylist.' But he is actually not fond of this title. The term 'stylist' could include a nuance suggesting that he is a director who is obsessed only with style or a blinded technician who fills the frame with superficial technique. Also, the term contains prejudice in its way of considering style and story separately. To LEE, neither style nor technique can have its own value in

My Bride, My Love, 1990

itself. His key interest lies in creating a way to handle and newly apply the technique, rather than relying on absolute effects. Whether the camera is fixed or on the move, whether it is captured up close or lit from far away, whether or not it uses a certain color tone, the style doesn't matter. 'Just as Monet portrayed light on the lotus rather than the lotus itself,' LEE tries to set up the concept for the film in his way rather than show character, story, a certain style or technique.

Let's take a look at his idea about the film set. He has not only filmed on sets many times, but also gained a high degree of know-how in terms of set application. Even if there is an art director involved, LEE designs the set by himself and decides how to use it. In his film, the set is not just a space where drama and characters exist, but also a story and a character, a concept, an element to reinforce or expand emotion. The layout, equipment, material and style differ for each concept. For example, in his film *My Bride, My Love*, an unrealistic set provides the space for the unfolding of the love story of a man and a woman. The honeymooning couple's house does not look like a real place. He visualized the sweetness of newlywed life through a vividly colorful space. The beach set in his film *Their Last Love Affair* visualizes the passionate love between two people who do not care about daily realities. Min-woo's apartment in the film *M* is designed in a dark tone to convey the inner state of a novelist in a creative slump. In all of LEE's films, the set is not just a location for events, but a flashpoint to decide the cinematic language and style.

Technique or style does not exist for its own sake, but is a means of showing a 'concept.' Having gained more importance in his films since *Nowhere to Hide*, 'action' can be viewed from this angle. 'Action' has a different concept from conventional action in LEE's films. His 'action' conveys 'the true nature of film.' He considers not action as an act, but action as a quality of movement and a way to show rhythm and flow. As well as using tracking shots frequently to convey the flow of the action, he also cuts and pastes shots together to emphasize the dynamics of movement. For instance, fast tempo editing conveys movement and flow. Generally, cutting means pausing or transition of action, but LEE Myung-Se makes movement through the rhythm of cutting. He also uses the terminology of rhythm, movement, flow and confrontation, instead of referring to 'action.' 'All film is action and all art is action. What isn't action when action is just flow? The movements of the characters, the movement of the camera and light—everything is about action.' Even the romantic melodrama *Their Last Love Affair* can be said to show the action of feelings. In this film, with lovers trapped in a love unacceptable in their society, the feeling of love is depicted with intense action such as fighting and lovemaking.

Nowhere to Hide and *Duelist* clearly show these characteristics of LEE's action. The former is not a conventional action film. An action film usually depends on suspense, but suspense is not very important in this film. Although LEE stayed with real detectives to collect their stories, this information was used just as reference material in his film. During his research period, a real criminal case unfolded and he was able to participate in the ensuing investigation. However, this experience was all just preparation to broaden his imagination. In *Nowhere to*

Hide, the action that he focuses on is the 'chase.' Simply put, it is a road movie about the journeys of the hunter and the hunted. Neither the motivation nor the reason for the chase between the detective and culprit is important. He intended to design a style of chase to convey the concept of 'chase' and focused on what is happening in the middle of the event itself. The significance in his film is placed on how the shape of movement, body gestures and action work on the mood and nuance, rather than on describing the movement in a straightforward manner. In the much-discussed final duel scene between JANG Sung-min and Detective WOO, the action is portrayed as the flow of image, rhythm and texture instead of 'performance.'

This was reconfirmed by the choreographic action in the film *Duelist*. LEE says, 'If *Nowhere to Hide* is about chase, *Duelist* is about confrontation. To show the 'confrontation,' action scenes were arranged with all of the things filling the screen set in contrast—man and woman, dagger and sword, vertical and horizontal elements. Theus, *Duelist*'s action differs greatly from those composed and elaborate action scenes seen in mainstream action or martial arts films. The movement was designed in each scene with feelings and rhythm; it has more to do with dance rather than swordfighting or martial arts. You can't find any particular martial arts technique or sparking between the fighting swords. Especially in the last scene, the duel between Nam-soon and Sad Eyes was styled as a dance or choreography of love, rather than just fighting between two enemies. To prepare for this film, the two main actors, GANG Dong-won and HA Ji-won, learned the tango and other dance steps instead of martial arts or fencing. Learning more than the basics of kung fu, Sun Moo Do (used mainly for defense), and break-fall, they learned various movements from masked-dance choreography, the tango, whose actions must be perfectly synchronized, and the finishing pose for throwing a ball in baseball. The special lessons the actors took implied LEE's different approach to 'action.' *Duelist* aims at a series of 'emotional actions' made up of movements and rhythm rather than the thrills of martial arts. The same can be seen with scenes in *Nowhere to Hide* such as the slapstick action, the 40-steps murder scene and the gruesome final duel between JANG Sung-min and Detective WOO. The scene was shot in the slapstick style of silent film, with almost no dialogue and with actions resembling a hide-and-seek game on a rooftop. The hyperbolic movement seen through the shadows and the dancer-like rhythmic action create a rather comic effect through the actors' bodies rather than a battle to the death between detective and suspect. Here, the action and rhythm can be seen as exploring movement itself.

Action as concept is not limited to physical movement. Every device in the frame used to highlight movement is an action. From the actions of a character and the actions of the camera to the action of snow, rain, steam, light and color, all of these are elements of movement and rhythm. The rain that pours down in *Nowhere to Hide* is a symbol indicating this movement. The lines of rain filling the frame during the final duel between Detective WOO and JANG Sung-min bring out the pure rhythm of the action. It's not the natural phenomenon of 'weather,' but the components of the frame creating a background and atmosphere. In this scene, LEE blends the camera movement with the movement of the rain. About this scene, LEE says, 'Rain is an excellent medium to show the way movement can be made essentially immovable.' The immobility he mentioned is not pausing in itself, but an immobility that contains movement. In this context, the reference to *jeongjungdong* used to refer to action in *Duelist* can also be understood. Translated, *jeongjungdong* means 'stillness containing movement.' It is the momentary state (pause) captured during movement (action). These two things appear to be opposites, but actually can coexist in one state.

Action is important even in lines of dialogue. For instance, the lines come rapid-fire when detective AHN and Nam-soon meet GA Do-chi for the investigation. In this scene, the actors recite their lines for the purpose of rhythm rather than pure meaning. This is also emphasized by the dialect used, which is intended to bring out the rhythm of words rather than to convey meaning. By relying on the accent and rhythm, the tone of sound and color in the scene combine with each other. The rapid dialogue delivered by the publishing editor, the father-in-law and Min-woo in the Japanese restaurant in *M* is another technique devised for the rhythm of language. The reason for emphasizing movement and flow is that it is another way to show cinematic time. Pause and movement, these are related to the nature of film as a medium. Creating a fantasy of movement using the linkage of photograms (still images), the film's mechanism consists of 24 frames per second. LEE Myung-Se inscribes this principle of pausing and movement into his films. It is for this same reason that images playing freely with the rate of frames per second are used for still cuts. A still cut appears during the conversation of Young-shin and Chang-wook at the farewell party in *First Love*. This shows the magical aspects of film in changing a photo into motion and at the same time directly reveals its illusive attributes.

LEE considers concept rather than 'technique' when creating a scene. The introductory action scene at the marketplace in *Duelist* is designed based on the concept of a 'duel amid chaos.' Even when a street fight starts over a bundle of money with the background vividly colored with fabrics, nameless flowers and colorful costumes, it is not important in the context of drama. All situations are organized to show the confusion of Nam-soon and Sad Eyes, falling for each other in spite of their antagonistic relationship. LEE makes full use of camera and optical techniques to create a concept. He applies techniques like iris shots, fades, wipes, dissolves and zooms that have been scarcely used since the time of silent film. Wipes in *Duelist* are used to show the movement of swords, and fade-ins and fade-outs in *M* are used to emphasize the opening and closing of eyes when dreaming. What is important to LEE is not the conventional effect these techniques create but how he can create a new concept by making use of these. The technique of the close-up is normally used to identify with or emphasize the character's feelings, but to LEE, it is a static technique. With regard to this, attention should be given to the close-ups of objects. The objects in his films are compositional elements that have as much feeling as the characters have. A vividly colored mug, a boiling kettle with smoke on the stove, an effervescent cup of soda, a stainless steel drum with the reflection of light from a train and cheap soap are not just items but objects with sentiment and emotion. When shooting a conversation between two people, LEE never uses the conventional system of shot and reverse shot. It is standard for Hollywood films to show the person talking from the point of the other's shoulder. But LEE mostly uses frontal shots of the one talking, which is considered taboo in

Duelist, 2005

traditional film production. This is due to the belief that, if an actor stares at the camera while talking, the audience will make eye contact with the actor and their secret identification with the actor—as they are stealing a glance—will be broken. However, LEE claims, 'If a stylish actor looks at an audience to talk, they will be more absorbed into the screen rather than distracted.'

LEE Myung-Se presents new ways of searching for the concept each time he makes a film. For films such as *Nowhere to Hide*, *Duelist* and *M*, which could be dubbed feasts of dazzling technique, it is no exaggeration to call them experiments to test his own cinematic concepts. His screen has an indescribable variety of both analogue and digital effects, such as high- and low-speed photography, oil-painting animation, after-image effects and extreme close-ups. *M* has a long-take scene, rarely seen in his other films. In the scene when Min-woo is meeting a publisher in a seafood restaurant, he is troubled with the pressure from the other man regarding the deadline for his manuscript. Filmed in a single take with no cuts, this scene portrays a stifling atmosphere to the point of claustrophobia, with a fan spinning out warm air as the camera hovers around the table. It is not the conventional function of the long take, guaranteeing continuity and unity of time and space, but an expressive technique to show the emotion and feelings of the character. By breaking down the conventional way of using techniques, LEE resists confining his film within established frameworks. He hardly ever gives direction based on a fixed script—the script is usually changed many times—and he also changes continuity from day to day. The objects in camera range keep changing according to light and darkness, subtle feelings of character or feelings of sunlight. By avoiding exclusive adherence to a specific style or schematization regarding the effects of style, he tries to prove that techniques are just tools to realize the concept of a film, without any absolute value by themselves.

About the MacGuffin of 'Story'

In one scene in *M*, the chief editor of a publishing company orders Min-woo to be 'less poetic and more specific' while urging him to finish his writing. These words seem to reflect LEE's own position when he was bombarded with criticism. The strongest criticism was directed at the weakness of his storylines. LEE Myung-Se was branded as a director who makes films with stories of little importance or stories that are all alike, in a time when talented storytellers abound. It's a 'fact' that he is not a brilliant storyteller. He has always been obsessed with finding the characteristics of cinematic language since he made his debut film *Gagman*. Admittedly, he has never been interested in the lively telling of a 'story' or a 'subject.' In his film, the main elements of the traditional narrative are just used as a pretext, or even ignored. Usually audiences are a bit embarrassed with the simple storylines if they don't pay careful attention to his films. The storyline in his films can be briefly summarized in a few lines, and even then they can sometimes have holes in their plots. Sometimes a situation can hardly be understood when reality and fantasy are randomly mixed together, while at other times the reasons for a certain situation are not clearly explained, or the actor's lines sound like a puerile love letter inspired by the feverish passion of love. There are storylines, characters and events on the surface, but they could seem incredibly monotonous if one just follows the flow of the story.

His understanding about film is to figure out the 'hidden intention' behind the story or face the essence obscured by the 'MacGuffin.' It is in line with a quotation from the French director Robert Bresson: 'The subject matter of film is an excuse for the style.' LEE once said, 'Film is all about the MacGuffin; it makes up a story to show something.' So the storyline, episodes, genre, actors and music are all 'excuses,' MacGuffins, that he mobilizes for what he wants to show. For example, *Nowhere to Hide* is a detective story. If we look at the plot, it is about a detective's endless search for a culprit. In terms of style and genre, it could be categorized as 'film noir,' owing to the characters being policeman and criminal, the numerous incidents at night and the particular tone of lighting in the film. But this is not everything. Considering that this film shows the path of detective chasing a criminal, it could be called a 'road movie' following a 'journey.' However, before anything else, it is a film about the energy of chase and motion, the creative and the primitive instinct of a human being. LEE investigates motion through the genre of 'action.' Thus he gives attention to the special nature of film not found in any other art, rather than a 'story.' 'Story' is only a pretext, a MacGuffin, to establish his film as a commercial one. There is more evidence of this in many scenes unrelated to the storyline: Mi-young's episode of a bus trip in *My Bride, My Love*, a backstreet scene to illustrate the passage of time in *First Love*, a harbor town with the high tension of a fight about to break out in *Their Last Love Affair*, and detective WOO's episode when he goes to his brother's house in *Nowhere to Hide*, all seem to intrude into the story with no relevance. Those scenes even seem to be taken from different sources and grafted onto the film. The intro part of *Their Last Love Affair* has an action-thriller scene instead of being melodramatic, and *My Bride, My Love* goes so far as to imitate a documentary. In the backstreet scene in *First Love*, the passage of time is shown in one cut showing a milk delivery man, a newspaper boy, a man skipping rope, kids going to school and a doctor going to work. Although it is far from the main storyline of Young-shin's first love, the sight of the backstreet visually portrays the passage of time.

Duelist presents a model case. As the film begins, a blacksmith recounts a piece of an unconvincing story. He says that a flirtatious woman asked him to come fix her copper chamber pot and seduced him when he came over. And then suddenly he screams and stops talking at the climax of the story. One might predict that a hot love scene would follow, but for no reason, the blacksmith ends the story and never appears in the film again. In a word, this is a LEE Myung-Se joke. It's his warning that the audience should not be captivated by a story from a storyteller. In other words, it's a warning that story is nothing but a MacGuffin. It's a declaration that he is not a novelist but a film director, and a film director is not a storyteller but a concept-maker within a motion picture.

What can be inferred from these scenes is the fact that LEE Myung-Se is only interested in an underlying 'cinematic essence' behind superficial tools such as story, character or genre. The 'something' hiding behind a storyline that is no more than an excuse or pretext is a different kind of pleasure provided by film art, namely complete the cinematic pleasure that is impossible to obtain from a dramatic story. Ignoring plot or character, LEE Myung-Se devotes himself to delivering the visual pleasure film art can create through image. As his films are filled with his desire to revive the expressive function of decaying motion pictures, plot is nothing more than a background to support the cinematic action, motion, color and tone. Everything he makes use of to create his own cinematic image or motion can become a MacGuffin. As MacGuffins, story, genre and actors cannot be overlooked, considering where film art stands as a popular art form. Audiences tend to pay attention to story, genre or actors (according to their recognition), but this director wants to show something different. This taste for fusing various elements instead of sticking to a certain story or genre inevitably detracts from the consistency of the storytelling. This is motion in *Nowhere to Hide*, 'cinematic action' in *Duelist* and 'light and darkness' in *M*.

Story, genre and actors are not the only MacGuffins; they also include all the materials he refers to. To live up to the title of 'integrated art,' LEE Myung-Se refers not only to art media, but also to sports and even the movements of animals. The action in *Nowhere to Hide* is intended to depict the essential and transcendent nature of movement through the intense movement of soccer players, and the scene of people fighting over a bundle of money at the marketplace in the early part of *Duelist* refers to an American football game where players struggle with each other over one ball. Like the oil painting animation in *Nowhere to Hide*, comic strips in *My Bride, My Love*, and photo montages in *M* and *First Love*, his reference material doesn't have any boundary of genre.

The Narrative of Images within a Weak Story

In terms of narrative, one characteristic of LEE Myung-Se's films is their episodic structure. It means that each episode is loosely connected to the situation without any close relations to each other, or that the story is happening by accident. *My Bride, My Love* conveys seven different situations for the story of a newlywed couple's most typical daily events and experiences, such as their wedding and honeymoon, the couple's argument at a house party, jealousy and misunderstanding. *Affliction of Man* also compiles single episodes just like *My Bride, My Love*. Depicting the exhausting daily lives of salarymen, the film is compiled of episodes by day—Monday is the story of a newcomer's first day, Tuesday of a company dinner, Wednesday of overtime work until the late evening, Thursday a karaoke episode, Friday the firing of a boss and the manager AHN Sung-ki running out of the office. Even though this film spares time and scenes to portray daily office life and intends to speak for the agony of men at work, it doesn't aim to stress the social issues that surround their lives, nor does it seek to educate. *Nowhere to Hide* as well is a story about a chase between a detective and a fugitive from justice. It makes an effort to visualize the relations between them, instead of describing the detailed procedure of the chase. Whether the film is about a lovers' relationship or employees' daily lives, LEE dissects everything with microscopic observation of their behavior.

His will to resist conventional dramaturgy is almost superhuman. The intention to break down the proposition that 'Film is a narrative art' is one of most prominent characteristics of LEE's film. Since the establishment of dramaturgy, the story has been the most influential means of drawing the attention of the audience. Film became story and story became film. If the genre of the novel represents the traditional narrative style, film was a child of modern narrative style. For this reason, film history has been written under the domination of narrative-centered films. Film became one of the greatest forms of modern narrative style because it developed the narrative by adding the aspect of an audience to the attraction of story. Furthermore, Hollywood has developed stories to appeal to audiences through its advanced process and has become a huge influence. However, can we say that film has always yielded to the power of the narrative? There might be differences of opinion on this. At the beginning of film history, before narrative-oriented dramaturgy had been established, people didn't go to theaters to find out

Affliction of Man, 1994

about stories. Audiences were enthusiastic about motion pictures in their early days because they were something magical, due to their lively movement. People were curious about moving pictures because the images that had been static before were now in motion and because of the visually lifelike movement. There was neither story nor character, only moving images to maximize the visual pleasure, so to speak. The original attraction of film can be explained by the visual power of image that instantly catches the eye.

Through narratives led by separate incidents and episodes that diverge from the usual development of the storyline, LEE Myung-Se tries to rediscover the original characteristics of the visual image through which film has fascinated the public from the beginning. The reason why people's souls were captured by motion pictures was not because of story but because of the movement of motion pictures, with liveliness unrivaled by any other form of art. For this, LEE minimized the controlling power of storytelling advancing through psychologically motivated drama and the rule of cause and effect by maximizing the mobility and energy of image. Cinematic imagism, gained after removing dramatic 'verisimilitude,' is the first model of anti-narrative style led by LEE. This tendency has become more pronounced in his more recent works. The cold reception of audiences to *Duelist* and *M* was due precisely to such prosaic stories. The viewers' disappointment with them stemmed from the noisy style, so giddy that it was hard to figure out a simple story or background. To viewers used to character- and drama-centered narratives, these films were merely dull films with stories that were extremely simple but unconvincing. Thinking that he included 'devices' but not 'explanation,' they criticized the films as having empty stories next to the idealized style permeated with the director's self-consciousness.

However, like the MacGuffin mentioned above, there is no other 'story' behind the story for LEE's film. It's not a theme or any kind of message he intends to convey by story. For example, the set-up in which Sad Eyes and Nam-soon fall in love with each other is important, but the reason is not. Likewise, the set-up of an undisclosed history between Sad Eyes and *Byungpan Daegam* is important; the details of the history are not. The set-up is meaningful because it can justify the vivid color performance, the camera's movement, the on-screen choreography, and the emotional action. It's the same for the motif of confrontation. There are two dimensions of confrontation; one is the confrontation contained in the plot between Sad Eyes and Nam-soon as chaser and chased, and the other is visual confrontation, namely of that between images, frames (montage) and among visual elements (colors, lines, movement). The former is not what LEE is interested in. It can have some meaning only when he considers how to express the latter well. The reason for this film being disregarded by audiences, despite being filled with the vitality of the moving image, was that the film didn't provide enough story to make it enjoyable for those who were familiar with the formula of narrative film (personality for the characters, an ending based on the rule of cause and effect, and story development).

To understand LEE's film, one should acknowledge that film has two narratives—narrative of story and narrative of image. Like story, image also has a narrative. The narrative of image is the logic of how to connect from one image to the next, between scenes, between colors and between the camera and the object. The narrative of a story keeps itself extremely simple, but the narrative of image is often termed 'stylistic excess' due to its expansion just before the saturation point. Without any interest in story, character or theme, LEE's films follow the movement of images, rhythm, color, and the flow of visual elements inside the frame rather than characters and events. Most of all, the elements in the frame move actively and are there to show their reason for being. LEE's film proves that editing can be determined based on the rhythm and flow of image, and not only on the story or the character's actions. Even if time and space change in terms of the narrative of story, the narrative of image maintains its continuity.

In order to accustom ourselves to this style, we need to be aware of things outside of the storyline and the existence of another track around the storyline. This consists of light and shadow in extremes to contrast the past and the present; the usage of colors; the camera's movement and editing, which destroys boundaries of outside and inside; and devices to visualize dream and memory. We must inevitably acknowledge the importance of style in that it focuses on the 'locutionary act' that is being narrated rather than the story itself. Perhaps silent film could be considered the most ideal form of film for him, without any prosaic conversation or explanation. This can be confirmed in the scenes where he shows silent film-style movement, continuing exuberantly from *Gagman* to *M*. In those scenes, all events stop and oneiric sequences reminiscent of silent film come into play. The scene where Detective WOO abruptly starts a snowball fight to distract and console his colleague, who has killed someone by mistake, in *Nowhere to Hide*; the scene of AN *Pogyo* investigating Nam-soon in *Duelist*; and the slapstick comedy scene at a seafood restaurant in *M*—all show a discontinuous rhythm that could be made only by LEE Myung-Se. This unexpected sense of rhythm differs from other, more typical films.

In order to maximize the symbolization effect of an image, LEE mobilizes every kind of device. Disobeying the system of entertainment established by traditional dramaturgy, his film pulls out from the process of delivering the pleasure of image by refining the plot and delves into the search for visual pleasure that is the mission of the cinematic image. This is based on his pet theory: 'If film isn't film, there's no reason to do it, and if film isn't cinematic, there's no reason to make it.' Pursuing the question of what cinematic movement, cinematic acting, cinematic flow and cinematic inspiration are, LEE has begun to reveal his obsession with 'cinematic movement and mobility.' At the base of this is the belief that it is oppressive to say that a film should be constrained only by the logic of the narrative.

One roll of film is the accumulation of various elements that cannot be restored merely through the story that forms it. However, it is no longer believed that a story can be replaced by senses, image and plot that cannot be verbalized. Whether proving the absolute power of the cinematic image or blowing a hole in the desire for narrative, such an attempt leaves audiences already broken in with the dominant film style of Hollywood unsettled. From this point stems the skeptical view that the dominance of narrative-oriented film will never vanish despite to the development of alternatives like storylines that are not fixed with self-evident meaning and plots that defy logic. Nevertheless, it is worthwhile that directors like LEE continue their experimental attempts to seek an alternative to those narrative films. What can differentiate film from other media is the quality of cinematic language. Cinematic language makes an 'auteur' out of a director. Material, story and messages have long existed, whether in novels or poems. How can a film be truly cinematic? To answer this, LEE Myung-Se challenges the absolute power of narrative as he tries to find a new possibility through cinematic language. LEE's films can never be seen as entertaining within a conventional appreciation that follows story and characters. The story is simple, the characters are not consistent and there is no message that could be called a 'theme' to pick up. They can only be entirely enjoyed when audiences feel the sensation grabbing them and the abundance of auditory and visual style.

First Love, Return to the Original Memory

LEE often describes himself as a 'chaser.' He is keen to chase concepts like the essence of film, life, dream and memory, in order to interpret them. All his films are about pursuit: *Gagman* for the identity of film, *My Love, My Bride* for marriage, *First Love* for first love, *Nowhere to Hide* for action, *Duelist* for movement, and *M* for the pursuit of 'dazzling' darkness. The targets he is chasing have connections with film, love and dream. Thus, LEE's films can be called 'love stories.' Even in *Nowhere to Hide* with tough detectives and criminals, LEE depicted a weird attraction between chaser and chased. Love is as important a subject for him as film, and 'first love' is the concept that forms the root for his films.

The last scene of *First Love* ends with the poem 'Ritual of Memory,' by the poet JUNG Hyun-Jong: 'After discovering the secret of the gold of time,/ Would you know the pleasure of it?/ At the beginning and end there is never anything./ There is only flowing between them/ The nature of song,/ The nature of cries./ Do not discard the emptiness./ Do not forget the flowing away./ Remember this:/ That trash is drunken on the ground,/ Stars are drunken in heaven/ And on the bridges in between/ You are bewildered.'

As we can discern from this meaningful poem, first love is an everlasting subject to LEE. If you need to pick one religion nearest to his outlook on the world, it would be Christianity. He has a Christian viewpoint in finding and reaching for love, but his method of considering the way to do so is closer to Buddhism. He is not keen to talk about falling in love, nor is he keen to look only at the relationship of love between man and woman. It's about a 'tao' (a doctrine of Confucianism) to reach truth or realization. His version of love is the same as what Confucius once described as truth or sincerity. LEE is continuously questioning himself while he makes films about love.

His third film *First Love* and eighth film *M* deal directly with the theme of 'first love.' It is known that *First Love* took LEE the longest time to write. He wrote the film himself, and says that he was desperate during the four months of writing. While falling in love for the first time is a universal experience, there's no general agreement about the meaning of the experience. After LEE reached the conclusion that first love has something to open the secret of time, he sought to reveal the secrets of humans and film in *First Love*. The essence of 'first love' is being aware of time past and the opening of the mind toward death. With his own theory about something we all experience but find hard to describe or explain theoretically, he portrays the sense of flowing life on the screen. *M* can be said to start from the ending of *First Love*. At the end of *First Love*, art college student Young-shin (KIM Hye-soo) travels to Seoul to meet Chang-wook (SONG Young-chang), who has gone to his mother's 60th birthday celebration. Young-shin feels her heart beating when she peers into Chang-wook's house to see the end of her love. The first love who stole her heart turns out to be a married man with a wife and child. Young-shin fights back her tears as she turns around to leave.

What would happen to her afterwards? Young-shin's first love left her and died. On witnessing the death of her love, Young-shin became a ghost wandering around the highest heavens. That's Mi-mi in *M*. Time passed and the first love was completely forgotten. The novelist Min-woo in *M* is the one who has forgotten all about it. Oblivious of his first love, he experiences writer's block. He has no inspiration and no ability to write even a line. It's all because of the disappearance

First Love, 1993

of the spirit of his first love. And then, Young-shin and Mi-mi return as ghosts in front of us. In our age, the muse of first love can only wander around in our lives as a ghost. First love cannot live, and can only exist as a ghost. Everything has changed. A lovely backstreet with a hair and laundry has transformed into a dark seedy backstreet with filthy wastewater or a sumptuous street lined with brand-name stores. Why did LEE try to create first love again in *M*? 'First love' does not mean only the first feelings of love. LEE Myung-Se presents what is felt in 'the process of chasing first love' and 'how to remember first love' rather than 'talking about first love.' If *First Love* was about looking inside the mind of a young college student who felt love toward her theater teacher from Seoul, *M* chases the dream of one man who retraces his memory of first love in the pitch-black darkness. His films on the topic of 'love,' such as *My Bride, My Love*, *First Love*, *Last Love Affair*, *Duelist*, and *M*, all deal with emotional elements like insecurity, neurosis, nightmares, sadness and regret. This portrays love as 'memory, emotion, mood and atmosphere,' not as 'story.' In the first love, first experience, first kiss, and first memory, the word 'first' has more of the concept of 'essence' rather than its literal sense. Love (first love) begins, and then vanishes. The set-up in which Min-woo feels someone else behind him while he is walking down the street relates to LEE's actual experiences (this experience is repeated through what Chang-wook says to Young-shin) from when he decided to become a director while he was in middle school. *First Love*, Young-shin and Mi-mi, and the first encounters with the ghostly first love are all threaded together in one loop.

LEE's film consists of a world where two concepts are engaged with each other and difficult to separate. His persistent chase for 'first love' is the result of his deep thought toward film. On the one hand, the chase for 'first love' is the same chase for 'the origin of film' and on the other hand, it is introspection on the essence of love, memory and death. First love is related to the desire for the origin. LEE's films all share his passion to go back to the origin of cinematic art, the origin of human nature, the pure state of the beginning. His ambition to regain the original magical character of film art also comes from this 'awareness of origin.' Just as he sighs over 'the loss of film,' nowadays film is becoming a 'ghostly art.' Like characters chasing for the ghostly first love that appears and suddenly disappears, LEE Myung-Se's pursuit of the ghost of 'film' is still ongoing. The thing is that his effort to revive cinematic remnants only appears in various genres and stories. The process of chasing the original love (*First Love*), madness and obsession with departing love (*Their Last Love Affair*), fresh feelings of love and marriage (*My Bride, My Love*), the pleasure of dynamic action (*Nowhere to Hide*), splendid audio/visual image and dancing rhythm (*Duelist*), and exploration of light and darkness (*M*): These films have all different looks, but they pursue the same thing.

First love is beautiful because it's hard to catch. It's not something you can pin down. Just as things fly away when we try to catch them, the momentary beauty is there with first love. That's why they say first love keeps a 'secret of time.' Time passes by anyway and is unstoppable. At the moment we say 'present,' the 'present' has become the past and the future becomes the present as time passes by. The concept is the same in first love. Film also has that kind of nature. Made of 24 still cuts in sequence to create an illusion of motion, a film runs unstoppable, flowing images, continuing heartlessly against your will when you want to stop one image. To LEE Myung-Se, therefore, 'filming first love' is namely 'filming time' and 'making a film.' In order to recover the sense of film and to make films with realization and feeling, the subject of first love means a lot to him.

The Myth of Integrated Film

While some make film like writing an article on a society page, and others like writing a novel, essay or dissertation, LEE turns film writing into poetry. Poetic words have a comprehensive 'feeling' and 'image' rather than fixed 'meaning.' When *Nowhere to Hide* was highly praised by Western critics, LEE was compared to John Woo or Wong Kar-wai. When he was highlighted as the first Korean director who would succeed in Hollywood, he became interesting to American and other Western movie people due to his talent for stylish action. His brilliant action scenes in *Nowhere to Hide* fascinated them. The people who summoned LEE to the U.S. expected him to become like directors from Hong Kong such as John Woo, Hark Tsui, and Ringo Lam, all of whom gained recognition making B-level action films and rose up to direct major Hollywood films. Rapidly-paced plotting and an extraordinary approach to visuals and unique heroic characters were the link between LEE and those others, but he was totally different from them in his approach to images.

For instance, LEE has a different approach when he makes an action film. In *Nowhere to Hide*, he creates a feast of plentiful colors through movement and light. Although I tried to find similar cases in Hollywood or Hong Kong films, LEE has strong elements that are uniquely his. For example, with the murder sequence at the 40 steps in *Nowhere to Hide*, the scene begins with a style reminiscent of expressionist film in the silent era. The murder scene occurs in slow motion in the street. And then the chase starts as blood sprinkles like rain and the rain flows over leaves. The scene does not elements that people usually enjoy in an 'action film.' There is none of the spectacular shooting, the physical violence of bodies colliding or the intense feelings imbued in the physical movements. Molded through arrangement and contrast of cinematic elements, it was more likely to overturn the existing sense about action film.

In this sense, silence in America might be predicted. LEE Myung-Se didn't go there to produce films at the request of film studios and work as a good studio director. Anyway, LEE couldn't live in harmony with Western producers or critics, and there was antagonism. He mentioned that Western views are trapped in dogma while he was talking recently about the critical response to *M* at the Toronto International Film Festival. After watching *M*, foreign critics labelled him a 'film fundamentalist.' With no way of being interpreted as favorable, this rhetoric means that he is a fundamentalist who has a blind faith in the value of 'essence,' like a Sunni Muslim who holds to strict Islamic principles. To this judgment LEE sharply raised his sword in confrontation. He confronted the claims by saying: 'OK, I am a fundamentalist. I believe film has a foundation and I'm willing to adhere to that value.'

Claiming that '21st century film has to be reinvented and further evolved,' LEE aims at so-called 'integrated film.' Integrated film can be defined as true 'comprehensive art' putting forward various elements of art. When we call film the 7th art or comprehensive art, it is supposed to regenerate the inner concepts contained in those words. Poetry, the novel, music, choreography, the theatrical play, photography and painting are all distilled in his films. He doesn't draw lines between anything such as East and West, man and woman. The frame in the seafood restaurant in *M* looks like endless photos without boundaries between their inside and outside. This kind of tactic is related with LEE's unique world view, which bends time and space, memory and dream, fantasy and reality. He does not acknowledge divisions between inside and outside, here and there, woman and man, or realism and expressionism. It's LEE's grand ambition to nullify every division and integrate art, philosophy and aesthetics. With his own perception toward realism, he destroys the boundary between realistic and cinematic space. The context of erasure of time and space in his films reveals his commitment to integrate everything. He would like to find the 'essence' that can be remembered even if time or place changes rather than a story that applies only to a certain time and place. The country town in *First Love* doesn't really exist in Korea. The beach where the lovers whisper to each other in *Last Love Affair* is an imaginary place, which cannot be found easily within reality. *Duelist* has a story where it is difficult to suppose what era it is taking place in. The spaces in *M* are also conjured by the imagination, given no certain time or space. For this reason, some criticize his films as stateless, artificial assembly products. His films mainly have stories that happen 'somewhere' to arouse cinematic feelings or 'at some point' in some unknowable time.

His criteria for locations are no different from this. When he chose Incheon to shoot the last action scene of *Nowhere to Hide*, he explained that it was because the scene was beyond any time and space. This is why he is unconcerned with differences between fine and pop art and also does not hesitate to appropriate things from other artists. It is the same with the boundary of tragedy and comedy. Both *Gagman* and *My Bride, My Love* are disguised as comedies, but are actually closer to tragedies. Humor is a tool to communicate concepts quickly and effectively. It's not that he applied a commercial strategy, but he does not deny that audiences tend to find more comedy than tragedy by their own will.

LEE Myung-Se's integrated film theory reminds us of French film critic André Bazin's 'total film' theory. In the chapter 'The Myth of Total Film' in his book *What Is Cinema? (Qu'est-ce que le cinéma?)*, Bazin pointed out that film is a realization of people's longstanding belief in the reproduction of reality. Even before the camera was invented, humans had the aspiration to reproduce reality, and this enabled the invention of film. As an integrated art, film can be called the most evolved art form, aggregating various streams of reproduction art. LEE never hesitates at anything when it comes to creating images. Paintings, photos, cartoons, music, documentary, philosophy and even sports can be references to him. *Nowhere to Hide* frequently uses images from oil paintings, and the chaotic marketplace scene in *Duelist* can clearly be associated with painterly images. The photo hanging on the wall in the seafood restaurant scene in *M* was inspired by Duane Michals' photos, and *First Love*, *Duelist* and *M* each have scenes looking like a configuration of Michelangelo's 'Creation.' Whether it was intentional or not, LEE reveals his ambition to integrate things that have been accumulated throughout art history.

Due to this kind of ambition, he is often pointed to as being excessively experimental. With their whirlpool of indefinable images stupefying the audience, *Duelist* and *M* left viewers in confusion. The sense of reality becomes more faded, and the abstract beauty of style is intensively shown as if to prove his belief that 'the only truth is the truth in film.' In terms of evolutionary theory, film is still an art in its embryonic stage to LEE Myung-Se. He says that it is 'just now starting to babble and toddle.' It can still be developed infinitely in the future and it has a language of treasures to be discovered. LEE says that it's the director's mission to discover and dig up those hidden treasures. There are more and more blank spaces in LEE's film. He says it's an artist's duty to knock on the door from behind to allow audiences to meet the film in their own way. In other words, it's a director's duty to draw audience into the film so that they can fill in the blank spaces themselves rather than to tell stories.

It is true that LEE always questions film from the basics. What he has pursued has been film in itself, and this started from his awareness of a certain crisis in modern film. Sometimes what is important to him is not the position of film in the field of art, but the exploration of the identity of film. Made with delicate direction, imagination and a craftsmanlike self-awareness, the 8 films that represent the fruit of his labors are outstanding for their unique quality, which had been absent in Korean film. He seriously casts the question of whether any film knows its functional principles. For the essential question of what film is, the answer differs for each artist. To LEE, it is an 'original' experience differentiated from previous art forms and it is also a belief that this is guaranteed by its original attributes of language. His continuous questions and efforts to answer prove that this stubborn film director is still on his way to completing his own world step by step. If we didn't have LEE Myung-Se and his controversial films, Korean film history would be more monotonous and weaker. LEE has taken on a unique position in Korean film for the last two decades. His efforts to free himself from the pressure of traditional realism and to get closer to the 'essence of film' distinguish him from other directors. LEE must have been born to make films and he will die with film someday while struggling to find its language. Thus, he is a 'cinematic human,' a 'Homo cinemacus' of our time.

Interview

Interview

You suddenly decided to pursue filmmaking while you were walking on the street at age 17. How did this thought occur to you?

SONG Young-chang once spoke about the situation in *First Love*. It could be anyone's experience. You suddenly feel like someone is following you and there's no one when you turn around to see. I had that feeling at that time and everything around me disappeared. I was with my mother then, but I was so scared that I just ran to my house. I had a very simple life until then. My wish was humble like anyone else's, which was to live well with my parents. However, from that moment, I started thinking seriously about things, like how would it be if my parents have nothing to do with me, or who are my friends, what is life? At that moment, the director character from the cartoon *Ddeang-i and the Movie Director* flashed into my head. 'Oh, I have to become a movie director.' But you know, I didn't know what a movie director did or how to become one. Considering this, I see myself as very reckless, crazy. (laughs) I was not into movies before that.

It's a rare kind of experience even for artists. What was the first thing you did after that revelation?

I immediately asked my mother for some money and went out to buy myself two books. Constantin Stanislavski's *An Actor Prepares* and the poet KO Un's *Biography of LEE Jung-seop*. I don't know why I bought them. I might have been influenced by *The Moon and Sixpence*, which I had read when I was in junior high school. Nowadays I think it has something to do with genetics. The constant belief that a human being has a hereditary mind must have attracted me. Both Gauguin in *The Moon and Sixpence* and LEE Jung-seop led lives of struggle. I decided to live with hunger. It seemed fascinating. I might have unconsciously believed that the director's life in *Ddeang-i and the Movie Director* was cool. That belief became linked with Gauguin's life and others and came as a 'sign' to me. How reckless it all was.

Had you had any particular connection with movies before that?

I was more into cartoons than movies. Many days in my childhood were spent in comic book shops where I could read comic books all day long with pocket change. I disliked robot cartoons and animal cartoons. I didn't like romantic ones, either. I liked so called touching, light-hearted cartoons. I needed only three won to read comic books for a whole day. When I was an elementary school student, I went to one of the comic book shops early in the morning with three won I had saved. The shop owner was preparing his breakfast and I started reading comic books. I intended to read all the cartoons in the shop that day. I even skipped meals and going to the toilet. But I was finally shooed out. The angry owner almost implored me to leave, saying 'Hey, kid! Aren't you going home? We need to sleep!' As far as comic books are concerned, I might have read far more books than Confucius did. (laughs) My mother used to make me notebooks with recycled papers, and I drew cartoons on them. I never brought drawing paper to school. I made drawings for my classmates and got drawing paper from them in exchange.

The funny thing is that the things I drew from them received awards in the competitions, but the drawings done in my name never did.

Considering the fact that you were a cartoon maniac, a lot of cartoon-like techniques are found in your filming, editing and scene divisions. *My Bride, My Love* or *First Love* reveals that kind of influence.

I can't say my childhood experience with cartoons lasted up to when I began filmmaking. Any true artist would try to find a universal way of expression. You could call it the 'essence.' The simple forms Picasso adopted from African art were the results of trying to find a universal language. How cartoon became one of the universal languages in my films probably has something to do with my encounter with Rimbaud's poetic theory. Rimbaud claimed that the era of universal language would come, saying that universal language could be found in lyrics of outdated popular songs, old magazine covers or cartoons. In the same context, I chose cartoons as a universal language. Realizing that cartoons can portray things beyond what film can reach, I came to adopt cartoon as a way of expanding filmic language. Of course, I don't deny that my childhood experience with cartoons somehow overlaps here. Actually, with all the questions I had on the methods of expression in cartoons such as exaggeration and omission, I could do many experiments on how to apply them to filmmaking. And it was all about finding a way to a universal language.

How was your college life as a film major at the Seoul Institute of the Arts?

People thought I was arrogant and stuck-up. Even nowadays people tell me the same thing, but as a matter of fact, that is all intended. It's like driving me into a corner. If I brag about myself to others, I would have to behave accordingly. That way I have no other options but to discipline myself with reading and studying. My ignorance helped me a lot. When I entered college, I was so ignorant and had no idea about movies. So I made it my habit to buy books whenever I could afford to.

From the moment I decided to become a director, 'What is film?' became my topic question and I didn't want to be a director until I got the answer. I made a list of several prerequisites to becoming a director. I would need intuition, insight and culture. I felt like I would have to know about psychology, sociology, aesthetics and everything. I tried to read, think and define as much as I possibly could. Meanwhile, all my readings and thoughts focused on what film is. I had only one guiding principle, which is from Baudelaire. His principle was to think only about poetry 24 hours a day. And I decided to think only about film 24 hours a day. I thought about film when I woke up. I thought about film until I went to sleep.

So did you get your answer?

A realization struck me. It was when I was working as an assistant director for *HWANG Jin-ie*. It was 12 years after I had decided to be a director. It came like, 'Yeah, that's it. That is what film is all about.' It's hard to put into a few words. It's like putting together all the questions I had been asking myself until then. Film is a truth, film is a way, and film is something we chase after. I just take the path. I'm free toward film more than anyone else. I haven't studied abroad and haven't seen a lot of films. People say this film is great and that film is no good, but I don't know. I mean, no matter how much people like it, it's nothing if you don't feel it yourself. It was when I was working as an assistant director on *HWANG Jin-ie* in 1986 that I became freed from all those rules and criteria of beauty and ugliness.

Does it mean that you got to conceptually clarify film?

Right. I create words and concepts. If a question like what a blank is occurs to me while reading, I start speculating about ways to make a blank in my film. Color tone, still-pause-move, rhythm and all concepts are the same. They are all created on my own, not from any aesthetics dictionary. With this rhythm, I make movies. My eyes for film have opened like that. And it happened all of sudden. I enter into movies through concepts. It's like, if I have a question about what a comma means, then the question continues to what a comma would mean in films.

You worked for 10 years as a production staff member for the director BAE Chang-ho. 10 years of apprenticeship should be long enough to make you a guru at a filming site, I assume?

I met BAE Chang-ho in the production team for the director LEE Jang-ho after I graduated from the Seoul Institute of the Arts. Chang-ho was the second in the team. I decided not to speak a word for the next three years after I started in the team. I don't know what was on my mind then, but I just decided that. I had been so reticent that LEE Jang-ho once told people that he would buy drinks for anyone who could get me to open my mouth.

When you worked as an assistant director on BAE Chang-ho's *Our Sweet Days of Youth*, rumor had it that you had much influence from that movie.

I just did my best as an assistant director. And BAE accepted my opinions, so the credit should be given to him. I started directing actors from *Hwang Jin-yi*. I would complete the setting and direct the actors. Then BAE would check out everything and start the shooting. Every final decision was made by BAE Chang-ho.

When you started your career as a director in late 1980s, the Korean film industry was dominated by political movies called the New Wave. However, your debut film *Gagman* is very different from this current.

'New Wave' was a name given by foreign film people. At the time, Korea was going through democratization, and intellectuals felt they were under social obligation. I had a different viewpoint on military dictatorship. I detested it because it destroyed people's imagination rather than because it oppressed democracy. It nipped people's thoughts in the bud. Since most Korean films introduced abroad at the time dealt with political issues, the world could get only a limited glimpse of

Korean films. So people got surprised when I went abroad with *My Bride, My Love* for the first time. They didn't know that a film like it existed in Korea. In Europe at the time, the left wing was predominant and perspectives to analyze films with were biased. I just made a film with what I was able to express through film. But I received huge criticism. Korean New Wave film was inseparable from the social situation of Korea at the time. Korea was in the transition period shifting from military dictatorship to democratic civilian government. Korean films, up until then, didn't dare to portray social issues in a straightforward manner due to strict censorship. Then a group of directors like JANG Sun-woo and PARK Kwang-soo appeared with the banner of socialist realism and critics in those days called them 'New Wave' to distinguish them from previous Korean films. I made debut around the same time they did, but my films were not recognized by many critics because my films were individualistic ones isolated from society. One critic even wrote that directors like LEE Myung-Se must disappear from Korea. It's rather unfortunate that I am categorized as New Wave mainly due to foreign critics. Thanks to them, my films could gain attention from local critics, and it continues up until now.

Your approach to image is different from other Korean New Wave directors. How would you describe the difference?

I never said that I was different from them. Maybe it came from critics. They found that my films were different from other Korean New Wave films. But if I have to point out a difference, it would be a difference in the perspective on film. I always have curiosity about 'Who talks about film as film?' Despite the fact that film is a new medium, it is still considered a branch of literature, painting, theater and photography. Even though every director starts from the same line with a question of what film is, some directors see film from social perspective and others see film from the perspectives of literature or other art genres. But I raised questions about film itself and have made each film as a way of answering those questions. The questioning is still ongoing. For instance, what is a close-up? As important as it may be, couldn't it be a toxic shot also? Then what is the proper way to use close-up? What is the distance of camera? What is mise-en-scène? Is it not a rule for people's lives? What would be the answer that only film can give? All these questions are the foundation of my films. This could be a difference if you ask me.

You have made many films that try to escape from the regionalism of Korea. It seems like a manifestation of your desire to find a globally universal 'language' independent from regional limitations.

I was looking for myself. I'm like a ghost. Foreigners ask me lots of questions about identity issues. They begin questions about my films by first pointing out that I'm a Korean and a male. But I'm not a Korean. I'm not a cosmopolitan, either. And I'm not a male. I'm not a female, either. I'm a ghost. I decided to be a man who wouldn't belong anywhere as well as could belong everywhere. So I'm not bound by any identity. Well, I still think about it, but it doesn't matter much to me. My concern is to find something that never changes in the flow of history. Unchanging things like the '108 torments of mankind.' So I believe that we have at least 108 types of subject matter to use, whether we're writing a novel or a poem or making films. This is why I erase time and space in stories; they are meaningless. The fact I live in Korea, in this present era, doesn't have any meaning. Assume that we lived in the days of the Japanese invasion of Korea. The key issue should have been the relationship between Korea and Japan, but it's just a page of history. Whether the story is about the Japanese invasion or the Gwangju Massacre, I would look for a certain story that would not change and have meaning for all. I might put in something to build narrative structure and to get the audience's attention, but that's not the essence of what I do. I once told this to a friend of mine who makes documentaries in Europe, and he was shocked. He said to me, 'Most Korean film directors have carried the burden of history, but you are different!' Is that really true?

What motivated you to make *Gagman* as your debut film?

Originally I was working on a film called *Family* for my debut. It was about a story of a father. Everyone liked it, but nobody wanted to produce. One day I had a dream, and in that dream, the word *Gagman* was written on the blackboard. So I wrote a screenplay about it. Many people compare *Gagman* with *Butch Cassidy and the Sundance Kid* and *Bonnie and Clyde* but I have never seen those films. Instead, NAM Chul and NAM Sung-nam (a Korean comedy duo from the 1970s) were on my mind when I was filming it. I followed a rhythm. A story about companions who pursue their goals without consideration of the situation of the day or humanity. It'll work, I thought to myself. I choose things considering the trend of the times. After I saw a gagman in that dream, I thought that was it. I wanted to make that film in a more serious tone and manner. The scene where LEE Jong-se robs a bank is the same one in *Nowhere to Hide*. I once considered using the song 'Holiday' by the Bee Gees, but it didn't match the feelings of the scene.

Gagman was produced by Taeheung film production. Did they accept the project from the beginning?

President LEE Tae-won is an interesting person. He turned down the project first time, but when I went to see him again, he just said, 'OK, let's just do it.' He has an extraordinary sensibility. He didn't decide by reading the screenplay, but he got interested after I told him AHN Sung-ki and BAE Chang-ho would be in the film.

The first scene in *Gagman* has the soundtrack from *The Kid* by Charlie Chaplin on a plain screen. It looked like sort of a statement to use Chaplin's music on LEE Myung-Se's film.

It was like destiny. The musical director of *Gagman* was KIM Soo-chul, but what he suggested was not compatible with the scene. But he said it was already recorded. So I tried to find some similar music, and then the Chaplin music caught my ear. In those days, there was no video equipment I could test. So I just used my imagination to design and edit sound to fit into the scene. The result was as good as I thought it would be. I didn't use his music at all.

Gagman has a lot of elements from Chaplin movies, such as a vagabond and a person in trouble caused by misunderstanding...

When I watched the film *Limelight* later, I found so many common things that are the strength of a Chaplin film. It was like this. When you think a man is throwing up, he is actually opening a bottle of champagne. It was the same way I did the opening to my scenes. It is probably a trait I inherited. I think Chaplin helped me a lot. I decorated the interior in one scene with posters that were a free gift from a movie magazine. There were many photos of Chaplin. By the way, the people in the photos hanging in the publisher's office in *My Bride, My Love* were all my favorite auteurs, like Rimbaud, Baudelaire, and Dazai Osamu.

Wasn't it Magritte's painting that appeared in the movie in *Gagman*?

Magritte is one of my favorites as well. The scene itself feels like a Magritte painting. Although it looks like a door, it is not, and the wall is not a wall at all. That's what I realized. People tend to look at what it looks like but that's not all. If you really open your eyes, you can see something else. So what matters is whether your eyes are open or not. I kept my eyes open and suddenly could see after a while. But it doesn't mean that I couldn't see anything. It was just that my ears start hearing. Everything is the same. When your ears and mind are open, it means people can communicate with each other. It's a gene in your mind. When people have the same mind for each other, it means they are open to each other.

Gagman LEE Jong-sc wants to be a director. Why did you choose a gagman for the occupation of a person who wants to be a director?

Like Bergman's art theory, it is like reeling out a thread from a ball of string.

Anything could come out in the end. It could be an elephant or a rat or just a thread. It's similar with the way I write screenplays. I don't expect anything particular like the tail of an elephant, but just chase and follow to the end instead.

The first scene in *Gagman* is set in a barbershop. The barbershop is important and impressive as a space. The whole movie can be interpreted as a daydream in a barbershop. The barbershop appears both in the beginning and ending scenes, but it is a space with mixed reality and fantasy. It seems to function as representative space for the whole movie.

Unlike nowadays, I used to write screenplays like this. I would keep thinking about one thing and when the other thing occurred to me, I would follow that. I wouldn't sit in one place to calculate things like Hitchcock; I would just keep thinking. In order to move to the next scene, I would keep thinking. Then something would come across, and somehow, it was right for what came before. And I would pause again to think and the next thing would come up. But nowadays this way doesn't work. Since a few years back, I haven't dreamed anything to use for film. At first I was afraid, but these days I just collect images and take them apart. After this, I wait until those separated images eventually connect to each other.

Obviously, *Gagman* contains your personal thoughts about film and biographical elements. For example, the long take of the beach scene directly conveys your connection with films.

It just happened. As my own life was off the wall, it naturally got absorbed into the film. It's like adult person sitting next to kids in cartoon shop. The movie was cranked up one week after the screenplay was completed. So I could fully concentrate on filming, and it was finished within 28 days and 23 shoots. I just went for casting and filming. I don't think preparation is important. If I had prepared more, it would have been more sophisticated. But then I thought, it's my destiny, and went on filming. Otherwise I wouldn't have made it. That became a good training experience for me.

Who was the first to suggest casting director BAE Chang-ho in your film? Not only was the idea fresh, but most of all, his acting was brilliant too.

I gently persuaded him while I was working on the screenplay. Chang-ho has a good talent for acting. I wanted someone fat, but I couldn't think of anyone. Even though Chang-ho is a director, he is a celebrity, so I asked him for help. It worked because he also wanted to try acting. He was more of a planner than the others and proved to be multi-talented.

Your earlier films, including *Gagman*, were mostly shot by the cinematographer YOO Young-gil.

He was very meticulous with the lighting. Based on my experience with him while I was an assistant director, his cinematography feels like something is missing but still gives you a warm feeling. A lack of something but a warm feeling matched

Gagman, 1988

well with my stories. Since I had worked with him from my days as an assistant director, it was quite natural to continue the partnership. I had many arguments with him. It was a hard time back then. Hard work, low pay and excessive schedule pressure... So I tried to avoid the film crew and not face them when they were frowning. I said to myself, 'Don't look back! If you do, you'll turn into a pillar of salt!' I have a lot of heartbreaking memories. When we were shooting for *Our Sweet Days of Youth*, YOO said to me, 'I'll be damned if I ever work with you again!' And he said the same thing when we were working together on *Gagman*. And he has continued to work with me. I would have worked with him on *Nowhere to Hide* if he hadn't been ill. He is a really good cinematographer. There used to be several good cinematographers, such as JUNG Il-sung, SEO Jung-min and JUNG Gwang-seok. But now it's a pity the lineage has ended.

Did *Gagman* see divergent responses after release?

There was no controversy. I later found reviews by KIM Tae-kyun and KANG Han-sup. No one else seemed to bother writing about it. It was just rediscovered as a cult item or something. Perhaps it was due to the success of *My Bride, My Love*. One of the popular misperceptions is *Gagman* was a big failure at the box office. But the film had an audience of more than 40,000 at that time. In those days it was break-even if the film amassed 30,000. Since the film didn't gain much attention when it was released, it was seen as a failure.

The beach scene where LEE Jong-se mumbles about his dream was filmed very uniquely. It seemed reality and fantasy were mixed together, and the scene where MOON Do-suk accidentally shoots and kills a car repairman gave a strong impression. The backlight and the clash of sound and image were boldly expressed.

I wanted to add more lights, but the quantity of light was insufficient. I wanted whiter, shinier moonlight, as if snow had fallen. But with the lighting of the time, it was impossible to express what I had in mind. For the beach scene, we found an unfrequented place and did the shooting in a hurry. I don't even remember where it was. Hitchcock is an unbelievable man. He remembered every location. I don't have that kind of memory.

In the beach scene, LEE Jong-se mutters to himself in an exaggerated manner, 'Who will make a true movie!' Do his lines reflect your thoughts?

They were completely nonsense. I had never seen movies like *Sorrows in Heaven* or *Gone with The Wind*. I don't consider lines in a film to be important. They are just a means to create a feeling or an atmosphere. Regarding lines, I sometimes have conflicts with actors. When shooting *First Love*, I thought certain lines of SONG Young-chang's were not that important. So I said to him, 'It would be OK if it feels like, or sounds like, poetry.' But SONG took his lines too seriously and suggested his own version. Well, if it is a book, it's quite another story and lines should be important. But who would remember lines in a movie? What's important in a film is atmospheres and feelings. However, people like to listen more nowadays, so I'm trying to reconsider.

What were the things you thought as important in *Gagman*?

My thoughts on film. I consider important something under the surface or between the lines, because what is seen is no more than a phenomenon. I believe that something between the layers can be delivered to an audience. That way it can survive and last longer. KIM Mi-sun, a journalist from *Road Show*, really hated *First Love*. But she said, a couple of years after she saw the movie, she was home alone after drinking, suddenly the scene KIM Hye-soo was riding a bicycle on her way home occurred to her and she became tearful. That is exactly what I made the film for. That's what I wanted to show through *First Love*. What may appear childish is ultimately what's inside us, and with the passage of time it comes as a totally different thing. So I said to KIM, 'You're the true audience.' That's it. Getting back to *Gagman*, a third-rate gagman happening to get a gun and commit robbery, that's just a story. But the important thing is what you feel. You feel that the beach is like a dream, or snow. It feels like a daydream or reverie in a quiet and empty space. A friend of mine told me he didn't go to work for three days after he saw the film. He said he suddenly felt his life was empty. Amid all that, a phone call came. He was a true viewer, too. I think we made some kind of movie. I don't know how it works. Many people say film delivers a certain story, a certain message, but I don't believe it. What kind of message could a film deliver? It all depends on the level of audience's cultivation and understanding. I just arrange many tools as a reminder, such as old music or the tone of the colors.

Your movies often have scenes estranged from the context of the storyline. The barbershop scene and beach scene in *Gagman*, the scene where Mi-young takes the bus to the end of the line in *My Bride, My Love* and Nam-soon and Sad Eyes' action scene in *Duelist* all look like scenes existing apart from the storyline. Also, the first scene in *Their Last Love Affair* gives the impression that it's more like an action movie. Why are you fond of placing in these scenes that break down the narrative?

Those scenes reveal the main sentiment as well as the essence I would like to show through the film. Such scenes are main sentiment in *My Bride, My Love*. It's the same with action scenes in the *Duelist*. Usually people set the story first and find spaces, but I go in the opposite direction. Consider it a new way of writing a screenplay. It's a way to show space. When I was thinking of Busan as the location for *Their Last Love Affair*, the first thing on my mind was such scenes. The general idea was to break people's conventional imagination about film and shatter their prediction before they come to see the film. It's like the beginning part, the 'da-da-da-dum,' of Beethoven's Fifth Symphony. It's not linked to the main melody, but it makes people pay attention, with this unfamiliarity and confusion that makes you think, 'What is this?' The reason the foreign film industry liked *Nowhere to Hide* is because the film is an interesting mixture of heterogeneous things that are harmonized in their own way.

Do you think unpredictable heterogeneous elements will bring certain feelings or experiences?

I think those elements are important by themselves. Following rules is not everything. For example, the rules of how to do things—soft background music, drinking coffee and a motel room—are not everything in melodrama. Unpredictable things can bring some tension. They are tools to let the audience watch movies in a new way without prejudices. But it's freer when they are there. I want to show there are many different ways to see a film. In the same context, I often let actors speak while facing the camera in dialogue scenes. Some critics called it Brecht's 'distancing effect,' but that's nonsense. How could it possibly be 'distancing' when a movie star talks to the audience? Suppose Marilyn Monroe winks at the audience—they are not 'distanced,' they're absorbed into the screen. It's only out of habit that we use 'over the shoulder' shots in dialogue scenes. It's not an absolute rule. No one would say it's uncomfortable for actors to talk facing the camera. Everything is an illusion made by habits. We are accustomed to those habits. People talk about the subversiveness of the story, movements, genre reversals, episodic style, format, structure and framework of my films. But few point out how much the camera flow has changed. You'll see those changes when you watch *M*

Even if you go against conventional methods, you should have your own rules. What would be your system or philosophy in managing images, if any?

As far as dramaturgy is concerned, the episodic formula appears to be a consistent element. So does the frontal shot. As the novelist CHOI In-hoon attempted, writing sentences with no spaces between the words would bring a totally different effect. Metrical sentences create rhythm. What would be needed for film to look like film and be interpreted as film? Something has to be subverted. All of film history has to be subverted. How conventional is the way we watch films? Everyone sees it that way, whether it's the *Cahiers du Cinéma* or anyone else. They're not up to speed with film evolution. When I visited France in the early '90s, journalists from *Le Monde* and *Libération* declared that 'Film is now dead.' I told them, 'No, it's just the beginning now.' It's beginning again based on the films accumulated by previous directors. Our senior directors have discovered the language of film. Our assignment is to reassemble it to find a new formula. It's been a preparatory period so far, and now it's the beginning. In this respect, film has not been born yet. That's what I think.

Then, how do you think films are being reborn nowadays?

There is still a dominant tendency to view films based on the diversity of the story and the subject matter. It's not right to view film in terms of diversity. People still go on about a message to save mankind within the scope of a story, subject matter and theme. As if cursed by some divine punishment, they are still bound together with message and theme. Nowadays I think there are more people who have different views. Among the reviews of my films, my favorite was a comment from one French viewer: 'A UFO in Film History.' Eyes that can confirm the existence of UFOs are what we need.

So you make film with film. What would be necessary to explain film with film? Does it mean the distinctive attributes of language and style?

It's not about style. I never have taken style into account. The subject is nothing but the tone of literary style. From the moment you choose a subject, it instantly becomes literary style. If a painter paints a woman, they can automatically decide whether to use the color purple or red. Eventually the painter will paint her color. Why do the women in Modigliani's paintings have long slim shapes? That's the literary style created by Modigliani. That's the theme and literary style in which Modigliani chose to portray women. It's the same with the colors of Matisse and the rhythmical style of Van Gogh. Van Gogh was known to have epilepsy. Whether he was drugged or whatever it was, his painting always had rhythmical beauty. Whether he painted sun or stars, everything was bound together with rhythm. That's the world through the artist's eyes. The essence of art provides the world expanded by the artist. Art is making 2 ears instead of 1 and turn mono sound to stereo to THX. This can be done by musicians. Painters broaden the vision of the eyes, and philosophers enlarge your desk drawers and your brain.

So according to you, a story or subject is just a tool and the attributes of the language, rhythm and flow are to be emphasized. However, isn't it true that the audiences are already accustomed to following the storyline when they watch movies?

I see that habit is changing bit by bit. It's not right to follow the storyline alone, since film is a kind of visual art. Image is formed by vision so that it changes something in the optic nerve. The fact is that there are already some image-oriented films, just not as mainstream. In this respect, what I choose would be genre. I try an easier approach through genre. For example, I prescribe a genre by saying this is a love story, a detective story or action film. This is one way I can be kind to audiences. It's the destiny of film to be popular art; it should maintain a constant relationship of tension with the audience.

While *Gagman* stemmed from your interest in films, *My Bride, My Love* seems to have more interest in life and love.

I told you all my movies belong to the 108 torments of the human. *Gagman* is a story about the false dreams of a human, and *My Bride, My Love* is about loving and liking somebody. *First Love* showed the first love that everyone has, *Last Love Affair* was about a love story we dream of, *The Affliction of Man* conveyed the ups and downs of an anguished life, *Nowhere to Hide* described a master who devoted himself to one thing for a story of pursuit, *Duelist* was another confrontation continued from *Nowhere to Hide* and *M* was about lost memory as well as the relationship between memory and the dreams we dream every day. These are all general experiences, stories about and for everyone. I like to tell people my stories using things that they have experienced and are interested in.

My Bride, My Love, in particular, has many cartoonish elements. Those scenes with the word balloons and the comic strip-style split screens are reminiscent of cartoons stylistically.

Everybody experiences cartoons at least once; whether they still read cartoons or not, I assume that there is no one who hasn't looked at one when they were a child. Even if you are now a fan of classical music or crazy about jazz, you must have looked at a book of cartoons at least once in your childhood. Even if we are more into high culture nowadays, cartoons were one of those things that used to attract us when our mind was still immature and childlike. Using cartoon style means returning to those earlier days. It's the same with radio drama as well. It looks familiar and yet unfamiliar and new when it's seen in film.

My Bride, My Love left a deep impression, especially with the atmosphere inside of the house or the isolated backstreet. The image or the feeling remains from the scene where Mi-young waits for Young-min to get off work at the entrance of the village.

Those are the sentences and words of film. I just need to express them cinematically. If a train is passing by, I shoot the light of the train, not the train itself. And I try to find where to let the light reach. And then I show the reflected light on a space or an object near the railroad. Even when our neighborhood is humble, it doesn't just look shabby; it is pretty and painted with colors. That's my idea and dream about the world.

Speaking of color tones, you often use vivid colors in your films. It's nice to look at when you put in various vivid and surrealistic colors, but some claim that it conveys less of a sense of reality due to the color.

Colors are also what I dream about. I always complained about Korean films with drab colors and no imagination. I thought, OK, you're showing a garbage can, but

My Bride, My Love, 1990

do you have to show it with so little imagination? What did the Bible say about the creation of the world? 'God made the world, and saw that it was good.' That's the eternal truth. What looks good and beautiful is good as art. So I use pretty colors. In fact, I have superstitions. If a fortuneteller says blue is good for me this year, I only use blue. The same goes with yellow or purple. It doesn't matter which color it is. I just hope that, if it's a certain shade of yellow, that it will remind people of one of my films. That's one of my wishes. I'm just aiming at an effect of being remembered through stubborn repetition (laughs). Purple evokes *M* and yellow will bring up *My Bride, My Love*. I sneak elements aiming at that effect throughout my films. You can't catch all the fish when you go to a fishery. Just like the size of your catch depends on your ability and patience, I want to make a film memorable for one thing even after a long time.

Do you think memorable scenes make a better film?

I think it's a film that develops and expands over time. It's the same with a book. I sometimes get inspired when I read a book again and see some parts that I underlined previously. And I get to underline other parts this time. It expands like this endlessly. A good book, a good film, a good painting and good art can be continuously expanded. What I thought I knew changes each time. In this context, Socrates' words 'Know yourself' could be the best proposition. Knowing yourself is about knowing that you haven't known anything so far. This would be the ultimate proposition in philosophy. Existentialism came from the thesis that the only thing I know is the fact I know nothing. A true film has to broaden the boundaries of we have already known, not through story or message, but through visual or auditory experience.

Your films often show mirrors or windows. Do you have any special reason for placing mirrors for self-reflection or a window to reflect the world in your film?

Not by intention, but they are clearly something from inside of me. I can see those kinds of things on the street. I stand outside and imagine who lives behind that window or who lives in the place with the light in the distance, or what they think about. I imagine that people are dreaming of love while I'm just standing there. So I'm interested in people's lives behind the windows and also interested in the sound from there. In that respect, mirrors and windows are important.

The characteristic of 'peeping' was best exemplified in your film *First Love*. I heard that this screenplay took the longest to write out of all your films.

I thought it would be easy at first, but it took the longest time. Maybe I didn't realize how big and broad the description of first love can be. You could just say that it took a long time for me to figure out that first love is also the secret of time. I saw a line written on a blackboard in my dream at that time. It said, 'First love is the door to the secret of time.' Once you get to know about first love, you can know everything about human secrets. As passion, childish letters, and infatuation keep you awake overnight, first love is a miracle. It's as miraculous as water that becomes wine. You don't have to eat. It's a miracle. It's like a religious experience. And most importantly, first love belongs to a young age. It doesn't come when you are in your fifties. You can only recollect days of first love. That's why it's the door to time.

The backstreet scenes in *First Love* were very impressive, with the images depicting the flow of time. The images compressed together flowing time, changing seasons, and the lives of those people. I'm curious about how you were able to shape those kinds of scenes.

Sometimes you just need intuition. Usually I don't refer to the screenplay when I design a shooting script. The screenplay is all set in my head, but I often rewrite it when I design the shooting script. There is a shooting script, but I don't just follow it faithfully. Every final decision is to be made on the film set through concentration. My way of shaping images is very simple and basic. I just sit down and meditate overnight. I just keep thinking and asking myself, 'So, what on earth is the next scene going to be?' With my eyes closed, I sink into it. It's pretty hard and tough enough to give me a headache. I spend almost the whole night like that. Sometimes it doesn't work even after I spend all night on it. I can cut and paste shots like anyone else. But it is hard to do something different. I can't ever live just like everyone else. No matter how long it takes, I just sit down staring at a wall, and I follow what comes into my head that way. The scene where Young-min catches mosquitoes in *My Bride, My Love* formed in my mind during this kind of meditation. At first, I thought about the flame of a matchstick. Then I speculated on what this flame could be and came up with the scene where he burns the mosquito. When you figure out the first shot, the next ones just follow from it. There is a reason why I can't drink while filming. When you are desperate to see something, it will eventually show itself. The films I know are like this and the ones

I realized are the same.

It must require a high level of concentration to come up with images through meditation.

If you give full focus, you can see other things as well. Along with the faces, you can see their destinies. It can take anywhere from several days to one month to design one shooting script. So I need to plan the shooting schedule by myself. I arrange scenes to be filmed mechanically up front and push back the scenes that need a lot of speculation. Since I'm the only person who knows it, I have to make the schedule. Images have to appear concretely. They shouldn't appear in drawings or pictures. They have to move. They become certain only when they're moving images. I used to sit down until they appeared specifically, but these days I can't manage to sit that long. So I try to make scenes with images that I just snatched out from meditation. It's the Zen way and Buddhist meditation. I try to see the real forms rather than just shapes. And then you can experience a moment where the boundary between film media and the outer world disappears.

I heard that *First Love* was planned as an action movie and the idea was changed when it was further developed. How can an action movie change like this? That really is a miracle like water becoming wine.

Initially, I tried to add some feelings of love to a gangster story. However, it was too vast a subject to contain within just a few minutes. So after taking out bits from the gangster parts, the first love became a larger portion. Maybe if I had kept the gangster story, the film would have been more successful at the box office. (laughs) My all-time rule for writing a screenplay is that only what I see, hear and feel should be written down, without adding anything I don't know. I always try to be aware of my strengths as well. So I made an attempt to describe first love. Throughout history, there have been so many stories about first love. For instance, *Romeo and Juliet* and *The Sorrows of Young Werther* are all about first love. We keep making these stories because they're about a time we've lost and can't return to. It can only be seen when you open the door of time. Once you open the door, you can see a page of history.

Even after you became a commercially successful director with *My Bride, My Love*, you took a different path than others. Was there any change in you after succeeding at the box office?

On the day I learned of the success of *My Bride, My Love* at the box office, I made a decision in front of the theater that I would not attempt to make any kind of new film for another one-and-a-half to two years. Period. It's my habit to make very simple and reckless decisions like that. The reason for fixing this period of timeout was to allow one year for writing a screenplay and half a year to one year for filming. I might have thought that I would be swept away by the success then. So I shut myself off from the people who came flocking in to suggest the next project and invest once I succeeded. And then I just stuck to film. Afterwards, I started to struggle to survive again. (laughs) By the time I made *Nowhere to Hide*, my life was a cycle of borrowing money and spending it all.

It seems like you intentionally sought to cut yourself off from the sweet success of *My Bride, My Love* or *Nowhere to Hide* at the moment of triumph. You left Korea immediately after the success of your film *Nowhere to Hide* when producers were just about to line up to invest in your next project.

I'm stupid. (laughs) I really wanted to study English at that time. Somebody told me that I would be able to understand English after just three months in the U.S., and hearing that I became convinced. Since I was going, I made a plan to see lots of films and study in the U.S. At that time, after *Nowhere to Hide*, Korean films were on the rise. If I had stayed in Korea I might have been able to buy a house or something. (laughs) Everything must have been an intentional choice of destiny. I thought, it's not the time to earn big money. How conceited I would become if I earned lots of money. I know myself. I couldn't do that even if I wanted to. I have to make films only. I might have made my own destiny to only make films.

It doesn't make sense to me that you exerted yourself too much instead of enjoying a momentary success.

We can't define people in terms of logic. I just look into the true nature, excluding any extraneous elements. We have to look at things without prejudice and without the things that have been made already. It's the same with art or religion. Who is this? Is he the son of Joseph? Son of a carpenter? No. He is Jesus Christ, the Messiah. He's the Son of God. It's a way of seeing things differently like that. Generally we see things and people in a pre-configured way. Our brain functions like this. But it's not the true form. We have to put together everything for the true form to be portrayed. What I mean when I say that I realized about film is that I realized that fact. In this respect, I was born in 1974 on the day when I decided to become a director. That was the start of my life.

Are you Christian?

My philosophy is based on Christianity. Whenever I delve into the origin of my beliefs, I always end up with Christ. The life of Jesus was brilliant, like LEE Jung-seop's. Jesus realized about life in his young days and died on the cross, which fascinates me. I think his life is wonderful. I like the artists who lived their lives like that. And those are people who achieved something. My true wish is that I can keep this little bit of luck just enough to continue to make films. I wouldn't dare to wish for anything more. It doesn't matter whether I have no car or no home, it would be enough if I can make films.

Instinctively, anyone would be interested in pursuing the origin and beginning, whether it's for film, life or religion. Your life seems to be filled with questions pursuing first love, the origin of film and the foundation of life.

At times I try to psychoanalyze myself, and what I have been obsessed with since childhood has been death. The subject of death has captured me since I was a first grader in elementary school. I don't know why it stuck to me like that. I just couldn't detach myself from death from the time when I moved to Seoul from Munsan. Film might be the warehouse for my accumulated thoughts on that subject. I don't know how it started. Just out of instinct. I have to question everything. Why did I do this? So I'm quite slow at getting things right. It takes a while to bring myself to realization, but once it comes, the next step moves quickly.

Since you delved into the idea of death since your schooldays, death as one of the '108 torments of the human' could make the subject of your future film.

I guess so. I would probably die after making one film about death. That's why I wouldn't dare to talk about death. In most cases of films about death, the director died afterwards. You know John Huston died after making the film *The Dead*, right? (laughs) Director LEE Man-hee passed away after completing *The Way to Sampo*. They must have felt some spirit of death while making them. I could feel it when I watched *The Dead*.

In line with questions about the origin and beginning, the image of 'The Creation' has been seen repeatedly in your films. When Young-shin and Young-chang touch hands for the first time in *First Love*, it creates the design of this painting. *M* also contains this composition.

Did it? I think there is something like that. Perhaps there are some repetitive scenes in my films. Therefore we are surrounded by 'the way.' We can see if we open our eyes, but we just don't. You like the feeling of wind on your face, so you drag the feeling into the film. In Hitchcock's writings, there's a story about lovers who hold hands while peeing. I thought it was so right—if they are real lovers, why would they feel ashamed? If you truly love someone, you can even kiss while eating greasy food. That was the starting point for *Their Last Love Affair*.

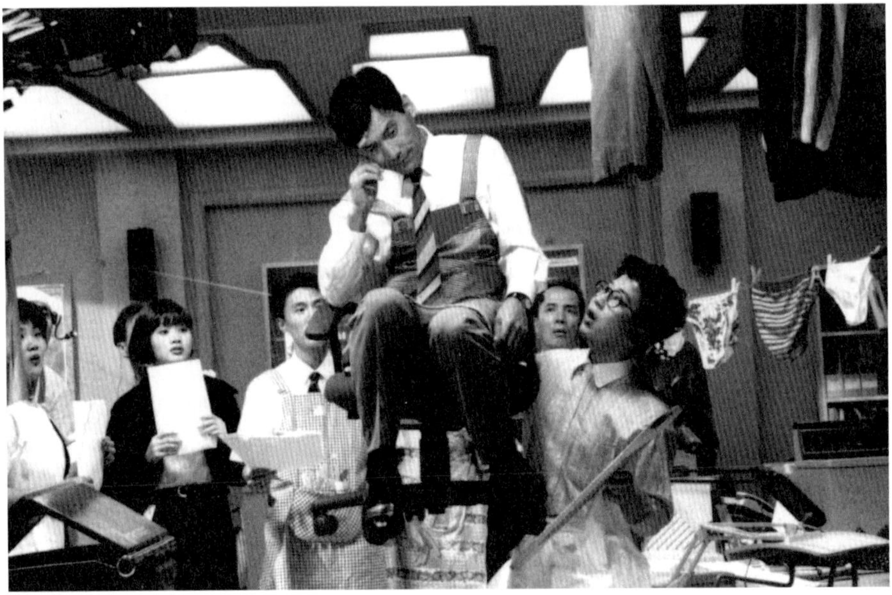

Affliction of Man, 1994

You continued to make love stories like *My Bride, My Love* and *First Love*, and then moved on to the story of the daily life of a salaryman in *The Affliction of Man*. The musical genre was also unexpected.

Some think I make films on impulse but actually I approach film with a strategic mind and plan everything ahead. All of the data I've amassed thus far would exceed that of any movie production company's planning office. I analyze the cycles of box office records in film history. I raise questions about films that vanished and think about how it would be nice if we could revive them. There are many suicide cases around the time I was making *The Affliction of Man*. I once planned a film called *Family*, a story about a father, before *Gagman*. It was a rather serious story before but I changed it while the actors were fitted for their outfits. Neither YOON Joo-sang nor CHOI Jong-won looked right in luxurious clothes. They were supposed to look like executives of a large company, and I wrestled with it for two days but couldn't think of an answer. The actors got annoyed, too, asking me what in the world I wanted. When YOON finally got annoyed and threw off his clothes in frustration, all his hair stood up from the static. At that moment, everything about *The Affliction of Man* flashed upon me. So I put a partial wig on him. The original title was *AHN Sung-ki the Manager* but Sung-ki felt awkward about having his name on the title, so I changed it to *The Affliction of Man*.

Was it your first time depicting only men?

I never exclusively focused on women either. (laughs) I tend to film as it goes so I never plan on limiting the story to men only. Some see *The Affliction of Man* as a musical, but I would rather this film were seen as depicting the joys and sorrows of working people through song. Initially, the scene where the salarymen become badly drunk had many details, but after I trimmed down those things, there were parts where it became more like slapstick and the musical elements came into relief.

The characters in *The Affliction of Man* are all named after the actors who play them. What was the reason for this?

It's all because I initially thought of the title *AHN Sung-ki the Manager*, and the characters' real names followed from that. Also, it's harder than you think to give everyone new names. (laughs)

In *The Affliction of Man*, day-by-day episodes are shown over the course of one week. With this structure, a comedy of manners quality emerges.

It's because salarymen usually move in one-week units. I thought that a week would be better than a month. It came out that way naturally after I collected some daily repetitive images. I think I started collecting images like that after I made that film. My films would be completed of their own accord from my collection of assorted feelings and images.

When you make the kind of form where images are collected, it's not shown specifically what kind of thing it is.

There is a story about Miyamoto Musashi in the book *The Golden Age of Zen.* There is a part about why Musashi can't explain his own sword skills. Why can't he write about swordsmanship without being philosophical? What makes his skills different from others? His physical swordsmanship can't be described in words. Musashi overwhelms the enemy with his energy beforehand. His winning is not because of his skills. He reads the mind and moves by his instinct. That's something similar. A moment can provide you with learning. He learned swordfighting skills by himself. Unlike other swordfighters who were trained to keep a certain distance from the enemy, Musashi never learned that. So he just threw himself at his opponents, and the people trained to maintain distance were surprised. He had an instantaneous realization, thinking, 'What's going on?' as he saw superior fighters caught unaware. From that moment, he could develop his diverse skills. That mindset is similar. The purpose is to cut the enemy's neck, and for that, rules don't count. I don't think rules are important either. If I were brainwashed for a long time studying, I would consider some things important. But I am not constrained in that way, so it doesn't matter to me whether I use cartoons or musicals. I just film it. (laughs)

It sounds like a liberal attitude unconstrained by existing dramaturgy or patterned rules became the basis for your filmmaking philosophy. However, the cinematic elements, the original things in films you proclaim, also seem to be made according to rules. Those classic rules were made by previous people in film history. Therefore I'm rather confused about your film philosophy and use of truly cinematic things.

We still can't define film with certain words. People are trapped in that respect. They don't understand why they have to use the fade-out. When a certain word was created, there must have been an essence—the reason why the word was created. But since the word has become standardized, the reason has been forgotten. I'm trying to find the reason and put things back together. I'm not saying that the things that are standardized are not film, but there's something real—an essence—which remains there in a dormant state. Let's take 'filial piety,' for example. What is 'filial piety'? Is it about being good to your parents? Or is it about bowing to your parents with respect every morning? It doesn't matter. I don't lift a finger when I go home. I just keep asking my mother to give me a meal, give me coffee, give me whatever. But it pleases my mother. I have an anecdote related to this. Someone went to Japan to see a guy who was known as being particularly devoted to his parents. Actually, the person turned out to be more immoral, more impious, than anyone, but his mother was really pleased with him. So the guy said, 'You're no pious son, you're a scoundrel,' and the other guy said no. What is filial piety? He claimed that the real conceptual essence of filial piety is just pleasing your parents. We are all tied to the notion of filial piety. Instead of looking at the substance and what is real, we just mechanically give money and bow to them, and we think that's piety. Some call that filial piety, but I have a different view. So going back to movies, people need to think about what a fade-out is, what a dissolve is, why you cut there. After you've been cutting for a while, you get used to it and it becomes a standard, and then it becomes a habit, but you mustn't think that it'll be a disaster if you break away from that. Nowadays those rules have become too solid and strict. We need to take a look at what we are missing. To pick one example, the dissolve and fade-out are supposed to be around two seconds in the optical process. If I suggest one second, or five seconds, the technicians will be strongly against it because it's outside of the rules. I say, 'Why not? Come on, let's just try,' and they just close their ears. They keep saying it's the time for the softest dissolve and the norm applied by many directors. What would make the number of seconds important? A fade-out is about darkness. It came from the concept of a curtain in a theatrical play, but it is about darkness in films. I think that moment of darkness is a scene in itself. It's not just a device for switching scenes. Here's where the difference is. I'm using the fade-out like this, but no one else would agree that it is a scene about darkness. (laughs)

Your films often have old-fashioned techniques rarely used in modern films. *Duelist* is a film of wipes. That isn't used as a general form, but especially with small objects, tools or an element out of the mise-en-scène. What's your reason for frequently using what might be called primitive optical techniques such as fade-ins and fade-outs, dissolves, and irises, along with wipes?

The wiping was used in consideration of the sword movements in *Duelist*. Since it was applied as if the camera moves, the speed and movement were very important. To show a change in scenes, I didn't use the concept of moving the camera's position, and instead I used wiping within a completely different aspect. I wanted it to be seen as 'movement' rather than 'a switch.' I also used a 'screw' form of iris technique with the movement of the washing machine in *Nowhere to Hide*. I don't stick to one old way to use iris technique. It would be the same scene if you used it differently. It's in my blood, a tendency to try different things. I was born to hate doing the same thing as everyone else. I always try to find ways to make it different. Ernst Lubitsch once said this: When he was co-working with Billy Wilder, Lubitsch suggested doing something different, whatever it took. Wilder heard this and did a lot of studying, and the ending scene of *The Apartment* shows the main characters playing cards instead of embracing each other predictably. That last scene, which betrays the rules of a last scene in a Hollywood film, could also be the best one.

The ending scene was special for Wilder, but in your case the opening scene looks more special. It looks like it exists separately from the main film. And as mentioned before, *Their Last Love Affair* looks more like an action thriller genre at the beginning rather than a drama, and the opening scene in *Duelist* unfolds with the tale of the blacksmith, which bears no relationship to the film's main story. Do you have any rule for making an opening scene?

I think of the beginning scene even before writing. It's vague, but I also have the last scene in my mind as well. The gap between them isn't structure, and has to be filled in during filming. Connecting the beginning and the ending is my style. *M* differs a bit on this point. I filmed the first scene as I planned it, but the last scene was changed. My writing style is to start from the first scene and continue writing to the last scene. I never set plot beforehand. It's the same with filming. I reassemble the shots after I've filmed them. Since I keep on imagining things, even I don't know what I'm filming sometimes while I'm in the process. It's not true that a filmmaker knows all about the film, which sometimes makes me upset. We might be more like translators, interpreting and delivering something from someone. I have thoughts. I say what I'm doing, but in the end things are made within a certain rhythm, a certain flow. It's not easy to fight against my will. This is how I make films. Creators are translators. Although we can think of something, it's essentially all made through communication. If I come up with the idea for a scene one day, it is just communicated from the warehouse of my memory. The whole process of filmmaking is about communication. It's similar to when you find every answer from a line in a book that you just randomly pick. Whenever I feel blocked, I just reach for something and find an answer there. That's communication. It's not like I thought about it when I picked it. Of course, I need to be ready with full concentration to take note of it. That's why I'm always afraid of the day when I might be unable to communicate.

Their Last Love Affair seems like a sequel to the previous *First Love.* Even though it's a fierce type of love, it has the passion and intimate sentiment of first love, which can be shared only between lovers.

That's true. The film started with a question about love. As a matter of fact, at that time I was planning to make a film called *Poor Lovers*, which was like *First Love.* As expected, no production company wanted to invest in it. Most everyone thought it would become another childish, corny film. So I ended up doing *Their Last Love Affair*, which was the screenplay I wrote before *The Affliction of Man.* One day, the novelist LEE In-sung told me about his novel *Imagining the Last Love* as he was getting ready to write it, and the title really hit home with me. So I asked his permission to use the title for my movie, but the word 'last' bothered me. What if this film becomes 'Imagining the Last Movie'? (laughs) And then my friend, the poet CHAE Ho-gi, published his first book of poems, which was called *Fierce Love*. The notion of 'fierce' is like a charcoal briquette. (Translator's note: The original Korean title of *Their Last Love Affair* means 'Fierce Love.') I chose this to mean colorless and scentless. I wanted to film interior and exterior scenes after building an open film set on the beach. There were some conflicts within the production team. The actress KANG Soo-yeon complained, 'Director LEE doesn't care about my pretty face, but is only keen on shooting things like the moon and cups.' (laughs) I ask to see the rushes, and I never show that kind of thing. I don't let people into the editing room, and I don't let them see. The producer couldn't see it, so he worried that I might make another art film destined to fail at the box office again. So he told me to come to Seoul, and I built the set and filmed there. I wanted to film under real and substantial sunlight, so it was a limitation for me to film on the set.

As the spatial concept changed completely, did it become different from what you originally intended?

No changes for the story or basic concept. I was originally going to tell a story where the beloved one would appear with a gruesome appearance after death. They say love and hate are two sides of the same coin, but it's not true. They grow on the same tree. It might feel more forlorn if filmed outside, but also more human.

There was some noise about the film set for *Their Last Love Affair*. You were taken as a crazy person when you made the film set a beach. The artificial set was misunderstood as the product of an excessively technical mindset, especially when compared with more realistic Korean films.

Realism has to be approached in a philosophical way. What is real? I think imagination and dreams can represent realism. It is a large category to cover. It's popular these days. I didn't mean to film *First Love* that way from the beginning. I decided to use a set after considering the location budget. A set is another means of creating a new grammar. It's like the effect of CG digital these days. If CG can broaden the imagination of an artist and make it possible to shoot from impossible angles, a set is the same way. It's a kind of expanded language. Something impossible for location filming in terms of camera movement and shooting angles can be made possible by the set.

Reportedly you initially planned an almost pornographic sex scene for *Their Last Love Affair*. However, the film turned out without anything that strong. Many scenes were suggestive, giving the impression that you weren't able to maximize the realism as you had initially intended.

When the film was distributed on video, a further 3 minutes of scenes were cut. I've always hated it when two lovers are usually seen covering their bodies when they get up from the bed in movies. I decided not to make those kinds of unrealistic scenes. No matter how naked you are, people in love don't get up covering themselves up with bedsheets. It's like that in realist film as well. In this aspect, I wanted to make a realistic film. When I said I would like to make a film with more flesh, like a soft-porn film, nobody believed me. They just thought LEE Myung-Se could only make another sweet love story, there's no way he could shoot any sex scene.

Your movies can largely be divided into two different periods. In the early period, love stories or daily life stories were the main plot, and later action and genre became more prominent. It seems like *Nowhere to Hide* was a turning point.

It's more about the difference between the 20th and 21st century rather than having any turning point. (Laughs) I had only two questions when I started making films: what is film and what is love. However, there's a limit to romantic films. Love stories don't seem to sell well internationally, so I strategically chose an action film. There were a few items I wanted to film. I've tried to forget those for a while because they're rather weak subject matter to go internationally. The reason why I aim at an international audience is because that's the only way to survive. I can do what I want after I make a foundation. So I will go back to love stories after I enter the international market. I also feel heated when I watch action films, but I prefer the sophisticated love story. It's also my strength.

How did you start taking an interest in 'action'? People were skeptical about LEE Myung-Se making an action film when *Nowhere to Hide* was released.

I wanted to make a film like *Memories of Murder* at first. I actually collected lots of data about the actual murder case in Hwaseong and made several visits to the town as well. I also met policemen and made arrangements to cast AHN Sung-ki, telling him, 'This is the next film, let's do it together.' Sung-ki waited for a while, and then got flustered after the film project changed and he needed to play a criminal who is not even a main character. He was shocked that PARK Joong-hoon would be the main character while he was in a supporting role. He later told me with all his heart that he even thought about leaving Korea at that time.

Nowhere to Hide was the watershed that distinguishes LEE Myung-Se 's 20th century from his 21st. It seems like this film brought your interest in cinematic action, movement and rhythm to the forefront. There was more camera movement and more dynamic style.

Nowhere to Hide was one of several screenplays circulating in film production for a long time. It may have been that people couldn't imagine me directing the film. On the surface, this film had a genre film framework that could appeal to the audience. The camera could follow the story, since there were detectives as main characters, incidents and action. The screenplay already had the power to make it. Actually, *First Love* also had movement and rhythm. There's constant movement there; it's just slower.

Nowhere to Hide, 1999

The duel scene of Zzang-gu (PARK Sang-myun) and Young-gu (PARK Joong-hoon) on the rooftop was very impressive. That scene must have adapted the shadow play from silent films. Afterwards, the tension between Zzang-gu and Young-gu as they're having a snowball fight disappears suddenly when the camera shows the next scene where the two are having ramen in the room. It's like you're confounding the expectation that something would be happening, but your film often has that set-up. The effect aimed at in these scenes could be what is called the pleasure of motion picture images. Why are you fascinated by these kinds of images?

The silent filmmaker's gene must be in my blood. I have no idea where it came from, but I guess late directors like Billy Wilder and Ernst Lubitsch helped me a lot. They applied those kinds of effects that were seen in the film. In other words, it's like showing some unexpected story after a funny part to elicit laughs. It's calculated direction that aims at unexpected effects. Irving Thalberg, who produced the Marx Brothers movies, once tried a stage test with the Brothers to see what people laughing at and how to deal with the laughter during the dialogue. When they needed to do some key lines, the audience wouldn't stop laughing. So the important lines couldn't be heard at all due to the laughter. Direction has to consider that kind of timing. It has to calculate the timing of the audience response. So you need to eat well before going to see a movie. If you have an empty stomach, you will think about having noodles when they're on the screen and you will miss the next several minutes engrossed with that thought. What you miss could be important. So a director needs to calculate that timing as well even when it comes to a food scene.

The performances and line readings of the actors, including PARK Joong-hoon, are unique. AHN Sung-ki and HA Ji-won in *Duelist* also showed that kind of acting. In particular, when AN Pogyo and Nam-soon went to question the culprit, they blew the culprit's mind with rapid-fire speech and non-stop movement, which totally destroyed the reality. It's the same with the scene in *Nowhere to Hide* where detectives question a culprit in the homicide team. Generally speaking, this acting is far from natural. There are often cases where they give mannered performances, with hyperbolic action and rhythmical lines.

It was supposed to be more mind-blowing in *Duelist*, but the actors became too exhausted to keep up with it. I wanted to capture the feeling of when the words blow your mind, but with movement. But since there is a limit with body movements, I used the sound clash instead. That was one of my attempts at literary metaphor. A 'pressing investigation,' how do I film that? How can I deliver the literary language in a cinematic way? After I worried about it for a while, that's how it came out.

In terms of cinematic rhythm, music is a significant element in your films. What are the methods you use or rules you consider important when using music?

Basically, I use familiar music. I think about connection rather than using one-off music in film. I would like the music to be associated with the film. It's the same with colors. I would like people to be reminded of a film when they see a certain color. I never use music just as it is; I edit it. I transformed 'My Dad's Youth' into jazz in *The Affliction of Man* and 'Sunrising Day' into rock music in *Nowhere to Hide*. I intended to break down prejudices about previously defined music genres.

The atmosphere in the 40 steps sequence and the action scene of Detective WOO and JANG Sung-min in the rain is quite electrifying. You once said producing such a scene is not from emotion, but is something like impressionism. Do you think this atmosphere is different from emotion? What would you like to arouse in the audience through these scenes?

I think the answer to this question would be a bit lengthy. It's because I first need to explain my own notion about language. Michelangelo once said that art that touches the hearts of people is not true art. People usually think the purpose of art is to provide touching moments. People usually say that they were touched by a film and that this film was the best ever. Also, filmmakers say they want to make films that deliver a deep impression on people. So this deep impression in the eyes of general artists and audiences would be false art from Michelangelo's perspective. Could this just be a language difference? In scholarly Buddhism, a human's emotions can be categorized into dozens of types. In this method, the deep impression that we often think of as an inner function of the human is categorized as a physical behavior. In other words, this emotion is also something material. In this view, it would be possible to understand Michelangelo's art theory. Art moves spiritual aspects, not physical aspects. Then we may wonder, 'What are the elements that reach out to the spiritual side of viewers?' Unfortunately, it's impossible to describe. Once it is put in words or described as a form, it can't reach the deepest part of the soul. In this sense, all of the things I show can't be anything more than an impression. What I'm really trying to depict is both inside and outside of it. However, if the impression is too strong, what I wanted to show will appear on the surface. Since I keep talking in an abstract way, I will make an example. Here we have two pictures of apples. Both pictures have apples, but in answer to the question, 'Which one is art and which one isn't?,' Khalil Gibran said this: One picture depicts just an apple, whereas the other enables you to see an apple orchard through the apple and to see God past the apple orchard. So the apple is just one form, one impression, nothing more than that. Apples can't be the theme. The apple exists only as one impression, and when the impression of the apple stays with people, it will lead people to the apple farm and the Creator God. This is my cinematic view.

Does it mean that art does not suggest a form but rather suggests a concept that merges forms?

It gets deeper as more films are made. All the commonly mentioned cinematic concepts will be tested and experimented with at least once. I test whether I can comprehensively harmonize artistic elements, dramatic elements and musical elements. It seems to be getting stricter. My ultimate aspiration is to make a film in which any one shot looks like fine photography. I believe that I have to reach that far at least. I'm trying to take on all of the terms in the cinematography book one at a time. What's a close-up? It's not a type of shot where the camera moves up close, it's a way of trying to catch close-up feelings. What's a full shot? What's movement or cutting? I will keep questioning and trying to find the way to use them cinematically.

Nowhere to Hide not only succeeded at the box office in Korea but also received high acclaim from foreign critics. As a result, this film motivated you to leave for the U.S. So what were the main responses you received from the foreign critics or media?

Jonathan Demme (the director who cast PARK Joong-hoon for *The Truth about Charlie* after seeing him in *Nowhere to Hide*) commented that the scene where PARK Joong-hoon was chasing after KWON Yong-woon was the best. The scene was my own answer about how to film the notion of 'chase.' People usually think of juxtaposing the two parts in a chase scene, but I wondered about how to convey the feelings of a detective's chase. So I tried a long-take instead of cross-cutting to film the chasing and running. If it weren't for the physical limit, I would have made it four minutes, but we cut it in half because they completely collapsed after two minutes of consecutive running. I would like to call it a new montage, without segmentation. I recently heard that the director of the film department at Moscow University said *Nowhere to Hide* could be a textbook for editing. I think it's quite a nice compliment to hear that from the birthplace of montage theory.

The chase scene looked like a kind of trick. The distance between PARK Joong-hoon and KWON Yong-woon seemed pretty far at first, but when the camera moved slightly, KWON was running in front of PARK's nose. I think the actors had to really consider synchronization of their action in addition to just running to match the speed of the camera movement.

Audiences know it all. If you divide it up to shoot, they will think you just pretended to work hard. I wanted to give the impression that we really worked hard. Mise-en-scène has to evolve like that. The tougher a scene is, the more I want to shoot it all at once, but it's impossible. So the filming started from sunset and went on to dawn the next day, and after all that I went with the first take. (laughs) So the actors usually complain a lot to me. When I was filming *Their Last Love Affair*, KANG Soo-yeon once grumbled, 'This is a love scene? It's gymnastics.' that the love scene looked like a mechanical gymnastic session. KIM Gab-soo, who played her lover, scraped up his knees crawling around on the floor of the room for so long. At first I thought it was red paint on the floor when he bled. Since I give the actors such a hard time, they usually say they won't ever work with me again, but they do anyway the next time around. To quote from a book by Billy Wilder, one actress's husband came to complain about her scenes after all her close-ups were edited out. He was angry. He pointed out that Marlene Dietrich was highlighted and his wife's face was cut out. 40 years later, the actress made a call to the director. She mentioned that she had recently seen the film again and thought it was great. Two days later, she passed away. It's an interesting story. Actors really don't know about it. I never let anyone—actors, cinematographers or music directors—into the editing room. They don't try to see the whole picture instead of just the part they are in. It's like pointing at your tiny face among the scores of people in a big group picture.

The frames in *Nowhere to Hide* are moved continuously, have their shapes changed or become fragmented. The same changes were made for the *Duelist*. What is your idea about framing?

I always emphasize one thing to the actors and staff before I crank up—not to decide anything. In other words, we shouldn't think that this has to be this way and that should be that way. It's because I believe that a film is a living organism. I also take the screenplay as a text we have to break apart. Nothing is to be decided before shooting. The plans you've made are there to be broken. It's not about filming things as they are. It's my style to follow feelings. With this as a premise, I try to have more conversation during filming. All lighting and sets in my films are designed by me. Since nothing is decided, it's hard to involve someone other than myself. Nevertheless, I don't forget the general premise of breaking things apart. Say that the key part in this film is stillness. However, my general premise would include breaking even this stillness.

You suddenly left for the U.S. after *Nowhere to Hide*. Due to its success both domestically and internationally, you gained a far-reaching reputation and many people tried to keep you here. Also, you must have been wooed in the U.S., but you eventually came back without making any films there.

I stayed in the US for around four years from April 2000 to April 2004. There were some proposals I turned down and some projects I couldn't get startard. One of them was *Check Freeman* but the main actor, Jeff Bridges, pushed me out, even after I suggested producing as well, since I'm a non-English speaker. He thought it would be hard to communicate with the director while filming, which is important to him. I should have made a film in the first or second year. I should have prepared more beforehand, but I didn't know anything. I couldn't speak English and the system was unfamiliar to me. Also I couldn't find any partnership, like Terence Chang and John Woo or Ang Lee and James Schamus. Maybe I could have settled down there with a partner who could play the game. Anyhow, I didn't reply to any calls from Jean Claude Van Damme, since that's not the way I wanted to make films. But that was my mistake. The system there is totally different from Korea. Since I was so new there, I needed to have a stage as a new director, which I realized after a while. I once told my agent that I wouldn't grant the editing rights to the studios, nothing more than mutual editing. 'I'm not here for commercial success.' It must have sounded ridiculous. I should have tried anything good, regardless of what the budget was. I was not supported by anyone at that time. So I finally decided to go back. After seeing the success of Ang Lee with *Crouching Tiger, Hidden Dragon*, I came to have hope that I could come back with a film made in my country.

What kind of movies did they request you to make in the U.S? Were they mixed genre films with Jean Claude Van Damme like in the cases of other Asian directors?

They were heavy action films. I could have made a simple film just to prove that I could adjust to their system. I gained some experience. I just focused on watching films as much as I could. I was really happy to attend the 'Film Forum' in New York to watch hundreds of films. I could call that my film school. I saw countless films by Buster Keaton, Fellini, and Jacques Tati, and I could see that they were all real film students. They were the ones continuing on the pulse of film. They were living students like the hidden apostles of Jesus. I thought, 'These were our masters and disciples.' Besides them, there were Kurosawa Akira and Stanley Kubrick. I'm also considering whether to include Bresson. I don't have a high appreciation for Orson Welles. His films are quite excessive. His films were approached with ambition and logic toward film. I don't think he changed film history. I just keep his film collection instead of watching it, just in case I want to check if he is also an alumnus of those apostles. (Laughs) I didn't change my style after watching those films. It's just about reassurance for what I thought.

You must have discovered many new directors for yourself, like Buster Keaton, whom you often mention.

The only Buster Keaton film I saw before going to the U.S. was *The General*. It gave me the impression that he made film as film. I was so surprised by his other film *The Cameraman* when I saw it in New York. A photographer sees a pretty girl and falls for her and tries to find out how to approach her. Since she is working at a movie production company, he decides to become a cameraman. He has no money, so he buys a cheap camera and starts filming. Even though he knows nothing about cinematography, what he films is pure poetry. I'm likely to cry when I see something beautiful. There was a piano player at the theater because it's a silent film, and the story was all told with one camera. It shows everything about film. I was so surprised by Buster Keaton. So I kept on seeing his other films, like *College*, *Seven Chances* and *Sherlock Holmes*.

How do you view Ozu Yasujiro's films?

You just need to see his film *Late Spring*. The ending scene, where there's a close-up of a father peeling an apple after sending his daughter off in marriage, proves that Ozu knows what film is. He knows exactly what close-ups are. All the other parts are condensed into this one scene. When he's peeling the apple, we can see through his life, through his feelings of emptiness and weariness. All of his life with his daughter so far and his own life are conveyed in that one close-up shot where he's peeling the apple. It's what we call a cinematic shot. One lonely man, a father, life—everything is seen in one shot. *Late Spring* exists for that one scene, which is the condensation of a whole life through a daily routine. It's amazing.

Spatially speaking, *Duelist* has a special depth in its action scenes—the marketplace or wall, for example. The movement is also directed back and forth. There were a lot of scenes with crossing shots both horizontally and vertically.

It was supposed to be bigger and deeper. There were problems with the size and budget. Owing to the limit, I was obliged to use the telephoto lens many times. I didn't consider the harmony of horizontal and vertical while I was filming. Van Gogh wouldn't have done that either. Depth is not made artificially but is achieved naturally through discipline. I do editing in accordance with breath and rhythm. There are no rules.

With respect to putting stress on breath and rhythm, your cinematic concept seems closer to music or poetry rather than a novel.

It's not necessarily true. I once tried editing while listening to music at the same time, but it didn't match the rhythm precisely. I just try to follow the visual feeling and breathing tempo. It's the same as erasing the sound completely and editing the visual only. My philosophy of film would sound similar to something from the Bible: 'And God saw everything he had made, and, behold, it was good.' When it looks good, I just go with it. Although I sometimes don't have a clear idea about things, I accept it whenever it looks good.

Some scenes in *Duelist* are reminiscent of *Nowhere to Hide*. The murder scene when Sad Eyes killed the Jongsa officer in the snow instantly calls to mind the 40 steps murder scene in *Nowhere to Hide*. Also, the scene where Nam-soon and Sad Eyes fought each other from each side of the colorful tents reminds us of the rooftop duel between detective WOO and Zzang-gu.

It was more about development rather than repetition. Originally, the murder at the steps in *Duelist* was aimed at creating a feeling of having the whole staircase disappear and dragging you inside, like a scene in silent film. But I couldn't make

Duelist, 2005

that kind of staircase, so I had to compromise with this scene instead. I couldn't achieve what I wanted that time, but in the next film I will search for more scenes that enable the concepts. That's how I can develop and evolve. I have the feeling that I need more specialists to visualize the scenes in my head. I need experts in various fields such as design and architecture. I agonized while filming *M* to produce effects with a limited budget.

There are many action scenes in complete darkness in *Duelist.* Surrealistic action occurs in pitch-black darkness, where all the surrounding things disappear completely. The best example of this would be the last scene where Sad Eyes and Nam-soon confront each other.

I planned that kind of scene for *Nowhere to Hide* as well but couldn't deliver it. I had the same picture in my head for the backstreet scene where detective WOO and JANG Sung-min were chasing and being chased. I would have needed a helicopter and a tremendous amount of lighting to complete the shooting. For the last duel between Nam-soon and Sad Eyes, I wanted to create an artificial perspective, but it wasn't good enough. Even when Nam-soon was chasing Sad Eyes along the wall, the space was supposed to widen and narrow, but I would have had to bring in architectural engineering equipment. It didn't come out the way I wanted. Given better conditions, I would be able to create scenes closer to my thoughts, and I would be able to try more things.

The movie production process is rapidly becoming digitized. Have you thought about making films using new technologies like digital or HD?

HD won't guarantee mobility. Its only real merits are the size of the camera and the cost of film. I keep my eyes on digital and HD. I can apply the technology if it's suited to the film. I'm old-fashioned, so I am fond of old styles like the Mitchell camera. Interestingly, American film crews in the old days used to work in suits on the set. They had to iron their shirts every morning like other white-collar employees. According to Hitchcock's biography, he used to have dinner with the crew or actors and things like that after filming. As part of his meticulous preparation, he also often brought boxes of wine to the film set and gave them away to the actors after filming. How pleasant it would be to have dinner with Hitchcock and get a box of wine. (laughs) In that classical sense, directors don't have as much authority as before.

As you said, when we define film as being about expansion and evolution, we usually can't find the meaning in general films that follow conventional ways. As a destroyer of convention, you create image-oriented films unattached to narratives. Your films prove that motion or flow do not exist in storylines alone, but also in images and the camera. Are you more interested in creating a sort of image narrative?

That spirit has already spread into modern films. Watching MTV and advertisements, I can sense that those ideas are becoming ubiquitous. When they point out that my films don't have a story, they seem to be adopting what others have said. People seem to be influenced by the opinion of others. The press and

Internet have an increasing influence. That's why we need critics. Isn't it a critic's responsibility to give meaning and find the point where a film is extending itself?

You often mentioned that film has to be simpler. What does it mean?

Simplicity can also be complexity. There is a saying in Buddhism. 'Emptiness is form, form is emptiness.' When you are not a hostage of prejudice, that's emptiness. From emptiness, you can see form. Form is what you can see after erasing everything. When you empty yourself, it becomes form. The true form will appear like a road appears out of the snow after it has melted away. Let's look at an example. There is an actor who always performs with very simple acting. People tend to think that his acting is very easy. For this, Billy Wilder once talked about how the people who get Academy Awards often get them playing people who are limping or feeble-minded or retarded. They only give awards to people who play parts like that. Looking at this, he said, 'It's the voters' revenge. That's the revenge of judges who don't have handsome or beautiful lovers in their lives, against the handsome, beautiful actors.' They want to give awards to someone who looks ugly and ignorant. They wouldn't feel good if they gave awards to gorgeous actors like Alain Delon, Tom Cruise, GANG Dong-won or JANG Dong-kun. From this viewpoint, SONG Gang-ho would be more likely to receive awards. You know, Alain Delon or Gang Dong-won don't look human. But the tragedy is, they don't understand how difficult it is to make something simple. It's the same as the difference between Western and Oriental styles of painting. Western paintings have many things such as story, color and layout. On the other hand, Oriental paintings are simple and empty, so something has to be added. It's difficult to see within the Western point of view. It's the same with films. Baudelaire once stated that a poet has to be a critic and he was criticized by people. But I agree with what he said. We have a tendency to arrange things into rules. Simplicity doesn't mean emptiness. There is an essence. It's about the realization of the moment you see. That's the essence that saves the Earth and human beings. I'm still searching for it.

You often give orders to actors to follow the camera, not the other way around. Normally, the angle would be decided by where the actor stands, but you place emphasis more on the camera movement.

We are likely to think the camera depicts actors. Paintings have frames. It's important how we design the space contained in the frame. So the frame needs to be harmonized with colors and other elements. It's silly to let the camera follow actors or have the feelings of the actors interfere with it. The camera is also an actor. Lighting can have a supporting role, and the space can be a performer as well. The question is, who is the main character? Actors also have to follow the camera and frame. They need to communicate with the other actor—the camera. We probably forget that we need to co-act with the camera as we do with other actors. Stanislavski's acting concept has been passed on to us. That came from the concept about acting and the actor in a theatrical play, not film. In the film *Ivan's Childhood*, Tarkovsky is known to have kept shooting a scene where a boy's shoe bag was taken away, in order to capture his anxiety. He was thinking how cruel the director's job is while he was shooting. Then the boy started looking around himself, rolling his eyes in anxiety. Then, can that be called acting in terms of classical acting theory? The point is the actor's mood needs to be right at the moment captured by the camera. That's the difference between theatrical plays and films.

Actors usually want to look terrific. Don't they hate your way of filming?

I can tell you a relevant case. When Hitchcock was making a film with Montgomery Clift, he directed him to walk and then raise his head. Clift was also one of the Method actors who studied with Stanislavski. Clift told Hitchcock that he didn't feel right raising his head. Then Hitchcock said, 'If you don't raise your head, how can I move to the next scene over the top of the church?' It's this simple. You can't keep looking down at the floor when I want to show some lights just because it doesn't feel right. It's a matter of transition—transition of places and shots. I can do a pan (panorama shot) only if the actor turns his head. I can't do a pan without some meaning. I always follow my intuition. How can I know all of why I have to place a camera here and move there? It's just because I like it that way. My decision is based on how good it looks later.

You mentioned using Buddhist methods and images. Could you fill me in more on this approach to image?

Simply put, it is the same with Gustave Flaubert's theory of 'le mot juste (the precise word).' The French writer Flaubert—he wrote *Madame Bovary*—claimed that any object should be described with just one precise word. I remember it's the same method that Henri Cartier-Bresson relied on for his photography. I also use Buddhist methods to adapt one expression for one shot. My method may be closer to Zen. It's about emptying all thoughts to gain one shot. It means that I throw away any prejudice and knowledge to focus on the object in order to gain the meaning that it's trying to express. It can be more easily explained by T.S. Eliot's theory about poetry. According to his theory, in order to describe a cue ball, you need to be inside the ball. That's exactly the Buddhist method I'm talking about. To do this, I first close my eyes to conjure up only darkness, and then wait until those scenes come and speak to me. So I think of myself more as an interpreter rather than a creator. However, not every scene comes to me this way. I sometimes write and make a film based on the general rules of filmmaking. But I found those scenes made the Zen way have always appealed to the audience. An arbritrary way can gain real empathy from the audience more than an artificial way. That's film, and it can't be replaced by any other art.

The main concept in *Duelist* was movement and rhythm, and it was light in *M*. What made you think about the creative use of light in particular?

It can be summarized as a 'dazzling darkness.' I don't know the meaning, though. It's a proposition from Heidegger. I'm still searching for the identity. It's not about highlighting the dark part in a scene. It's more like a philosophical proposition. It's embryonic. A light is there surrounded by darkness, which could be said to represent chaos or darkness. Isn't the state of youth a dazzling darkness? Darkness that bears light. There is light even though it is dark, like twilight. It's not about dividing the concepts of light and dark. I'm still chasing it. In the Bible, there is the sentence, 'In the beginning, there was light.' What is light? It reveals things, puts a name on things. Things exist when the lights are off, but it's as though nothing is there, and then they become visible with light. Conceptually, *Nowhere to Hide* was a chase for the chase, *Duelist* was a chase for the duel, and *M* was a chase for dazzling darkness.

M has often been called a comprehensive work of LEE Myung-Se. This sounds right, in terms of first love, memory, chase and the process of finding the secret of time.

It's a man's journey to find himself through his first love. It's a story about everything love contains. The slogan 'Looking for M' stands for this memory, this mysterious process. As a director, I can't help always thinking about 'movement.' It basically constitutes film, and film has to prove itself as a film using only this. We tend to think that proving this is like opening Pandora's Box. It's because nobody proves films as film. I'm not a scholar or critic, so I just keep making films.

Your new film *M* is known to have been developed from a screenplay called *Myriam* that you wrote in the U.S.

Many parts have been changed from *Myriam*. The location was changed to Seoul from New York and the main character was changed to female from male. It changed a lot, since New York and Seoul are different spaces in themselves. In New York, the light gets cut off or obscured by skyscrapers, and it isn't like that in Seoul. In Seoul, it's hard to find places like 42nd Street or 5th Avenue. With *Myriam*, I had the ambition of filming New York in a new style. But due to the spatial limits for *M*, I had to use a film set. So like *Their Last Love Affair*, which had to be changed when it went from being filmed at an outdoor location on the beach to being filmed on a set, *M* also changed significantly in that respect.

What changed after you decided to make the main character male instead of female?

The point of view changed. I had planned for *Myriam* to have Myriam's point of view, and *M* had a male point of view. Also *Myriam* was narrated by a dead ghost, while *M* resorted more to the imagination of a male writer with his point of view.

For almost all of your films, you design the production set by yourself. I was told that *M* was done the same way. I even saw you directing the set production for *M* after filming ended. It looks like *M* is a compilation of LEE Myung-Se's set aesthetics.

It's just the beginning rather than a compilation. I'm reevaluating the efficiency of the set. Sets are good for controlling light. It was important to make masses of light and shadows in *M*. That was the concept of this film. Since I have a clear goal of creating 'dazzling darkness,' I can simply separate where to put light or where to place darkness. What is the effect of set in terms of efficiency and aesthetics?

M seems to cross the genres of mystery, thriller, romance and horror. Why did you want to mix the genres?

We are trapped in a framework with regard to concepts like thriller, mystery and horror. Is a 'thrill' about trembling? It's the same with suspense. When the notice arrives in *Billy Elliot*, there is suspense, as we are curious whether it's a pass or failure. But we don't call it suspense, we call it emotion. It's all thrills and suspense. The word 'melodrama' comes from *melos*, meaning 'singing.' What about not singing? Is melodrama for crying and laughing? If it makes you laugh more, it's comedy. Can we say Chaplin's films are comedy? It's not right to follow an existing category. In this respect, I wanted to create the beauty, horror and thrills of an Edgar Allan Poe story for *M*. I wanted to express an atmosphere from Poe's stories by harmonizing various elements. I was speculating on whether I could do this while I stayed in the U.S., and from this *Myriam* was written.

Speaking of Poe, *M* has the plot of a detective story and a chase. Also, the spot where the writer and his lover from the 'old days' encounter each other is a bar called 'Lupin,' which is the name of a character from a novel by Morris Le Blanc. Why did you use this name?

There is a real bar called Lupin in Japan. It was the Japanese writer Dazai Osamu's favorite bar. There is a picture of the Lupin in his novel *No Longer Human.* I went to that bar when I went to Japan for the first time. It's a small bar located on a backstreet off of Ginza, beloved by Japanese writers. I found it matched up well with *M*. The strange thing is that I remembered that there was picture of Osamu hanging on the wall in the bar, but I couldn't find it the last time when I stopped by there while promoting *Duelist*. Clearly, it was in my imagination. When I asked the owner, he said there had never been any picture like that. I saw there were just small pictures hanging. When I asked if they had changed the lighting, the owner also said no. I thought that the experience was like the one in *M* and that a human's memory can be really mysterious.

I got the sense that your directing style for *M* at the filming stage had changed a lot compared to when you made *Duelist.* You seemed to listen much more to the suggestions of your production team. What happened to you?

Duelist was my first film as a 21st century rookie director, and *M* was the second. (laughs) I had learned much from my experience.

It is hard to figure out the whole plot and message in your films after one viewing. I especially got this sense with *Duelist* and *M.* It seems like your film has to be re-watched to get a real taste of your meaning.

I read *Romeo and Juliet* when I was a child, and it's still good to read today. As a grown-up, I can see more of the dialogue, sentences and philosophy. It feels different depending on when you read it, so much so that some people study Shakespeare for their whole lives. There are hidden treasures in fine films or fine art. Film directors can be surgeons for the soul and manufacturers of mental products. Film is not something just to let flow or let be. A book can change your whole life with one line, and film is the same way. Film can be like junk food, but that doesn't mean it's something to avoid—even with street food, it's different when it's produced with feeling and when it's just thrown together. Morality exists not only in food but also in films. Devotion is the bottom line, but it should be supplemented with flavor. And while you're at it, the display will make it even better. Why do they care about counting rice, like 200 or 300 grains, for sushi? It's because it makes it taste and look better. That's the path a master develops.

The main motif for *M* was dreaming. It's a story about dreaming, memory and love. Why did you make this complicated story that crosses between dream and reality, reality and fantasy?

Everyone has dreams. No one lives their life without dreaming. It's such an ordinary experience, but ways of dealing with dreams are not ordinary. Commentary on dreams comes with difficult theories from Freud, Lacan or Derrida, which can make the story more complicated. People have the tendency to think that daily life is separate from art. They think that films or novels based on dreams will be complicated and hard to interpret. First love is the same, when you ask people to consider it. I asked people when I wrote the script for *First Love*, 'What color would you assign to your first love?' Nobody thought about first love when they started their first relationship. After a while, they realize that it was first love. The first experience, first love and first kiss are all different, but they all get mixed up, and there is no clarification as to what can be called first love. First love is just compartmentalized due to the stereotypical portrayal in popular novels. So we tend to consider first love as an old theme, childish, but the secret of time lies within it. It's the most philosophical and Zen subject.

M, 2007

M brings to mind two things. One is your third film First Love, and the other is literal first love.

First love is the keyword of my film. This film is about a man finding himself through his first love. It's a story about pursuing everything that first love has. The slogan 'Looking for M' means the process of memory or mystery. Unlocking the secrets of time. There have been many stories about first love throughout history. *First Love* by Turgenev, *Romeo and Juliet* and *Sorrows of Young Werther* are all about first love. First love stories are popular with writers due to the fact that the secret of time is inside. If you open the door, you can see something. Something pure, nervous, and feverish and infatuated keeps you awake. Why can a person not sleep if they love someone? What they call lovesickness is a psychological sickness. It's miraculous. The moment of knowing first love is a moment of experiencing a miracle. It's like an eternal theme. It's the way I look at film and my first intention for starting in film from the beginning. Where did all the passion go? The thing I should not lose is the beginner's mind, the mind about film. I don't ever want to lose that excitement and infatuation.

Your definition of first love is related not only to the lover's relationship, but also to film and life.

In the end, cinema is doomed to be pop and plaza art. It has to find ways to appeal to more people. *M* actually contains my desire to expose my ideas about dreams. I sometimes dream things in advance. When my mother comes in my room to clean, I can see that's exactly what I just dreamed beforehand. So I know what my mother's going to do next. You could call it déjà vu, I guess. People say it's a silly dream, but I wanted to solve this question. I saw *Ratatouille* yesterday, and there was one line in it: 'Imagination will come to the one who imagines.' Dreams are the same. They're a gift to someone who believes in them.

Do you have any special memories about dreams?

The title of *Gagman* was written on a blackboard I saw in my dream. The word never occurred to me before. Ever since I started to trust my dreams, I have obeyed whatever I see in my dreams unconditionally. I'm a Libra, so I'm indecisive, but I never give up on what I have dreamed under any circumstances. Nobody can change my mind about the image I've caught after waiting with my eyes closed. I've also dreamed about the presidential elections as well, from PARK Chung-hee to ROH Moo-hyun. Whenever I've dreamed about who would be the next president, I've never gotten it wrong. I even predicted what percentage of votes President ROH would win the election by. Really. This is too confidential to speak about. (laughs) Whenever I've wanted to deny something, dreams have always proved the opposite and I had to accept it.

You keep awakening the idea of 'first love' due to the scenes from the past. The back street, bicycle, moon and fog are all objects used in the same way in *First Love*. Space and items that recall the past appear consistently.

It's for this same reason that people on bicycles appear once in a while. Someone said, 'To eat noodles with black bean sauce is to eat memories,' and I think it's true. As we get older, we find the old taste in our memory. I don't think old things are useless and something to throw away. I might be still fighting with the idea that such beliefs are old, false and nonexistent. You can't have even that value being false and fantasy. What is seen is not everything.

Since *First Love* failed at the box office, you might have wanted to prove your belief about it one more time.

I definitely did. Among the responses to the film, the scene of Min-woo and Mi-mi's first love in the old days was viewed favorably by almost all audiences. It tells us *First Love* is still effective. In 1993, people saw it and thought it was childish and embarrassing. We sometimes judge things saying it wasn't good at the time, so it's not good. In some cases, we need to withhold our judgment. Momentary judgment can be overturned at any time. If the scene of first love arouses feeling and empathy, it can be said that it wasn't a failure.

How did you shoot the scene where Mi-mi was kicking and struggling in the darkness while she was being chased by the Umbrella Man? It didn't look like CG.

It can be dangerous attempting to find out too many secrets about the film. (laughs) There were staff members working in the darkness as the Umbrella Man. It was quite a primitive method of filmmaking. I just wanted to express the feeling that the darkness was pulling Mi-mi. There was no meaning in particular. One of those things I hate the most is 'meaning.' The most hateful words starting with 'm' are 'meaning' and 'message.'

With respect to space, there are three back streets: A back street from the old days with the Mona Lisa hair shop, a high street in Cheongdam-dong, and the alley with the Lupin Bar. These are all connected to each other. The back street with the hair shop seems to have changed into the street with the Lupin.

When I planned to shoot it in New York, I wanted to introduce the downtown area of New York in a new way. But it's hard to shoot a whole downtown in a frame. After thinking about how to get the whole thing into one flat screen, I came up with the reflection concept. All of the back streets appear to be connected to each other. If you turn a corner on any downtown back street, you will find it leads to another, so they are all connected, aren't they? So I designed the space with the exterior and interior both connected. The concept was applied to Min-woo's apartment as well, so it looks like a labyrinth. It's like the backstreet and apartment are connected to each other.

There are unclear scenes with front and back reflections. The scene where Min-woo pushes the revolving door to go out onto the high fashion street and the scene at the furniture shop are like that. It was hard to tell what was the inside and outside.

Day and night can't be divided either. When I was doing military service, I was engrossed with the concept of outside and inside. I even decided to solve the concept before leaving the service. One day I had a daydream that I was in a castle for a party. The people started to disappear one by one, and when I was eventually left alone, I couldn't find my way out. I searched for a key but couldn't find one, and after wandering around for a while, I came up with the idea that I could simply break down the wall to let myself out. After I broke the wall, I could see people appearing one by one. But it was ambiguous whether I was outside or still inside. From there I was inside, and from where I was standing they were outside. That kind of concept. I couldn't figure out which place was closed or open. So I concluded that there was no division of inside and outside. It's just about division. So I came up with an appropriate conclusion, solved the problem, so it was time to leave the army. And that's how I ended my service. (Laughs) I believe that inside and outside are just a distinction, but they don't really exist. Only 'now' exists. There is no future, and the future means believing in the values of now. In terms of the concept of time, the past, present and future keep intersecting. It differs only when we view it with the concept of memory. In conclusion, there is only the 'present.'

M is your darkest film so far. When the past was contrasted with the present, the faces of the present were shot so dark as to be scarcely visible.

I intended to shoot in a darker tone but the lit part came out more in contrast with the darkness. The bright part seems to be brighter. I initially aimed at having only the first love part look bright. I tried to make it bright as possible, so much so that it really seemed like it would take off flying. On the other hand, the present should be dark. The high street where Min-woo was strolling actually needed to have more lighting. It was supposed to be the middle part where darkness and light are coexisting. Although it's a realistic street, it should have looked like a dream space, but there were some parts hard to express in reality.

When you look at the photo hanging in the seafood restaurant, there is no division between inside and outside. There are exchanges of roles and changes in the lines of the editor, father-in-law and Min-woo, and the sound also changes according to the wind from the fan. Even imagination and reality mix together.

It's a feeling of déjà vu. The seafood restaurant could be a very realistic place, but it gives a mysterious feeling. After agonizing about how to depict Min-woo's situation and the stifling feelings of repetition, I filmed it in one single take. I wanted to show the pressure from the camera as well. This film is about a man who is looking for his identity.

If *Duelist* is about wipes, *M* would be about fade-ins and fade-outs.

You might call the fade-in and fade-out something like eyes opening and closing. It's like closing or opening eyes when you dream or die. What would it be like to die when you close your eyes? The moment of darkness falling is the fade-out and the moment of opening your eyes to meet the light is the fade-in. There are two different types of fade-out: momentary and slow.

How does memory influence the present?

It makes us realize belatedly that there was something before. We don't realize a first love while we are in it, only later on. It doesn't mean that it was not there because we didn't know. It was obviously there and we realized it later. After something is gone, it feels truer. Why couldn't we realize that before? We need time. Art can remind us of some values we didn't care about at the time. It's art that knocks on the door and opens our memory. The Bible also says that the one who opens the door when someone knocks from outside will find a way to live. It's the artist who keeps knocking on and opening the door of memory. Some knock with colors, some with music, some with writing and some with films. There's no meaning to it. One of the most hateful words is 'meaning.' The most hateful words starting with 'm' are 'meaning' and 'message.'

M has a ghost, but there are so many scenes without boundaries of reality, fantasy and dream. Some scenes leave the viewer feeling confused.

It's a perspective I love. It's my perspective on dreams and life. Many of the questions in my stories show traces of time and the desire to grab hold of time. It feels like those stories are a permanent part of my movies. It makes me sad that life or love just remains as a fading memory. It's heartbreaking. I would just like to change those feelings into films. Questions about what life and death are continue to stick with me. As a result, my films have many scenes about dreams. Maybe all my films have at least one. *M* is the one that confronted the subject head-on. Dream sequences are an inevitable part of the film. What would the world look like to the dead? I feel discouraged by that thought even when I'm really into doing something. I start wondering about what I'm doing. It looks like a comedy if I step back and take a look at myself. But it will continue as long as I exist. This idea may have been embodied in my films.

Speaking of 'death,' the French critic André Bazin once associated the birth of cinema as a concept with death in his book *What is Cinema?* According to him, the origin of film is in the process of mummification from Egypt. A mummy is made to preserve a dead person from decay forever, and Bazin explained that it signified an urge to overcome vanishing and death. Calling it the 'Mummy Complex,' Bazin said the will to overcome death continued into the desire for perfect reproduction. As the most evolved form of reproduction, film is also motivated by this everlasting desire.

Love is another way to overcome death. The reason why a human keeps evolving is that something always looks good to them. It's a different concept from something that is simply born. Unlike other art forms that show one still point of motion, film shows it moving. If we think about the great development of humankind, we could be just single cells. Those cells fight each other and a certain gene will survive. And that gene will be passed to the next generation, and then the next. It's the same with the genes of a film. It could completely disappear when it dies, but maybe something will survive. So let's have an interview again before I die so something will survive. (laughs)

Biography

FOR THE LOVE OF

Biography

LEE was born the third child of two sons and two daughters in Asan, South Chungcheong Province, in August 1957. After an uneventful childhood, the first question that struck him was 'death.' He has been anxious to answer that question since he was in the first grade, but remained an ordinary student without any special interest in cinema until suddenly deciding to become a film director later in life. He watched and enjoyed movies like others. He doesn't harbor special memories about movies, unlike some movie fanatic who started watching various movies extensively from an early age. He doesn't remember anything special about his childhood except being really good to his mother.

What captured him in his childhood was not 'films' but 'cartoons.' Whenever he found time, he would go to a cartoon shop to sit down and read for several hours. He read a colossal number of books and he even drew some cartoons of his own. He was a talented cartoonist, and his cartoons were very popular among his friends. He claims to have drawn at least ten long-form cartoons by middle school, and he often gave his cartoons to his friends as gifts. Cartoons were one of the major things that dominated his mind to some extent during his childhood. He learned to read from a cartoon his older sister and brother borrowed from a shop, and aced his literature classes throughout his schooldays thanks to his learning of reading, writing and sentences from this genre. As cartoons, like film, are an art form with appeal through pictures and the visual, it can be regarded as an influence on his later interest in cinema.

It was not some inevitable incident that caused him to decide to be film director after spending a relatively ordinary life as a child; it was rather an unexpected moment of realization that came upon him. One day, in the winter of 1974, LEE Myung-Se suddenly decided to become a director while he was walking down the street. He recalls that he "suddenly felt the question 'What is life?' come upon me." It is a normal thought for any teenager to have, but he thought it over and decided to spend the rest of his life looking for an answer. Thus, he began to plan his future in a new light. LEE started to re-examine all the questions he had taken for granted so far. What is life? What is love? What is freedom? What is friendship? What are parents? He even harbored such odd questions as, "Could I reject a pilgrimage to a Japanese shrine if I had been born in the time of the Japanese occupation?" In seeking to find overall answers to his many questions, he started to think about how he was going to live.

The conclusion he reached after lengthy speculation was to become a 'film director.' Considering the fact he was not really interested in movies at that time, his decision must have been related to his fondness of cartoons. As he was thinking deeply about what he would become, the image of a director from a cartoon flashed into his head. A bald-headed, pipe-smoking director named NO Min-ho, from the 1965 cartoon *Ddaeng-i and the Movie Director* by LIM Chang, to be precise. From that moment, he intuitively made the resolution that he would become a film director. The story is also explained in the narration delivered at the beach by LEE Jong-se, the main character of his debut *Gagman*. Thinking, "That direction in the cartoon looks so cool," LEE Myung-Se arrived at the decision of hinging everything on becoming a film director. Even though it was a rather unexpected conclusion that came out of a long period of consideration, LEE kept on with his resolution to be a director.

He calls that moment in 1974 his second birthday. He was born in 1957, but he claims that he was reborn as a film director in 1974. In this respect, film director LEE Myung-Se is 34 years old. Back in those days, LEE didn't have any idea of how to become a film director or what the job entailed. This was natural, as he didn't particularly like film and had never really been into them. He just decided that if he wanted to be a director, he should enroll in film school, and he began watching whatever films he came across in theatres. He mainly watched Korean films, especially popular teenager films by KIM Eung-chun or MUN Yeo-song, instead of foreign films. At that time, LEE held MUN, who occasionally appeared on TV as well, in high esteem as a great artist. Trying to find his place in the world of cinema, he entered Seoul Art College as a major in film studies. He was in last place among those admitted. In fact, he barely made it in at all, thanks to one student who gave up enrollment for financial reasons. Even after he began studying films, he was no more than a film outsider. He couldn't help marveling at his classmates, who could speak about so many great films and recite the names of famous directors. During his time at Seoul Art College, he never stopped asking his essential questions. He would ask film students what film was, poetry students what poetry was, and literature students what the novel was. He is still asking himself these questions.

In those days at Seoul Art College, there were many well-known artists and people in the field of culture in the faculty. The novelists LEE Cheong-joon and CHOI In-hun gave lectures and the director HA Gil-jong also took part in lectures. Both directly and indirectly influenced by them, LEE Myung-Se also taught himself and began to find answers to his question: "What is film?" One of the biggest influences on him was critic PARK Pyoung-sik, whom LEE named as his 'mentor in films.' PARK Pyoung-sik used to use harsh words, and LEE, who had never had a formal film education and had little cinematic cultivation, was called 'ignorant.' Having a passion for study, he started asking himself what made him so ignorant, even if he hadn't gained much knowledge by then. PARK's harsh words stimulated and motivated him. He tried to read as many books as possible to cover the areas he hadn't reached yet. His own style of delving into problems stubbornly until he solved them gave him more discipline.

After graduating from Seoul Art College in 1979, LEE began staffing at film sites. He first joined the production team working for director LEE Jang-ho, regarded as the best at that time, but the production of the film *Sudden Flame* was suddenly canceled during filming, and he moved into the production team working for veteran director KIM Soo-young. Later, he finished his military service and searched for a career path while doing temporary work, like distributing movies in rural areas, before he returned to the film set. He then began working for BAE Chang-ho, and for the next ten years gained experience on his production team. During the filming of BAE Chang-ho's *Hwang Jin-yi* in 1985, he finally found the answer to his longstanding question, 'That is film?' He was very close to the successful celebrity director BAE Chang-ho, but he claims that they didn't have much in common when it came to filmmaking. LEE established his own view and philosophy about cinema and he was just waiting for the day he could prove something to the world.

His debut came with *Gagman*, but the film turned out to be a disaster. It was scheduled to be shown during the Christmas season, but as *Die Hard* became a huge hit for the distribution company Taeheung, the producers of *Gagman* decided to postpone it for six months. Ultimately the release date of *Gagman* was pushed back to a year later. The film didn't gain much attention either from critics or audiences, but it is now admired as a cult film by those who rediscovered this film later. After *Gagman* disappeared leaving little impression, LEE directed his next film, *My Bride, My Love*. It was a hit at the box office, and he began to be recognized by many people. It looked like he had finally hit the big time through this film, where LEE adapted romantic comedy in his own style. However, the '90s were a consistently tough time for him. One of the best reviewed of his films, *First Love*, failed terribly at the box office, and his next two films, *The Affliction of Man* and *Their Last Love Affair*, were also back-to-back failures. A rumor circulated in Chungmuro that LEE Myung-Se, an extremely obstinate artist, would bring failure if allowed to make films the way he wanted, and his name was added to a blacklist.

After struggling to find producers, he made a dramatic turnaround with his sixth film, *Nowhere to Hide*, exactly ten years after his debut. As his most successful film, *Nowhere to Hide* attracted attention as a challenge to the action genre departing from his previous subject matter of love and trivial everyday life. Apart from the point of differentiation with a genre that appealed to audiences, the film represented the best of LEE's style. Having by then built his own world separately from any commercial interest, he chose the action genre to survive in a commercial film industry. However, this choice also put him on a different path as a film director.

The success of *Nowhere to Hide* added his name to a worldwide list of remarkable directors. The film was not only acclaimed at the Sundance Film Festival, but was also highly praised by director Jonathan Demme, director of *The Silence of the Lambs*. After announcing LEE's presence at several film festivals, the film was distributed in the US. As a result, LEE also received proposals from Hollywood. Even though he had an established record for filming in Korea, he decided to go abroad to make films and moved to New York in 2000.

After four years in New York, he hadn't made any films. Several scripts were handed to him, including *Phone Booth*, but he was stubborn in his decision not to take the same path as other Asian directors in Hollywood. He would not give up editing rights, which he thought of as the basic right of a creator. However, it was not possible at that time for a Korean director to demand this right within the Hollywood production system, where the studio usually holds the editing rights to a film. LEE Myung-Se couldn't start any project for a long time. In spite of his initial intention to make films according to his beliefs in the foreign environment of the U.S., this time taught him about his limitations and lack of experience. He eventually returned to Korea.

However, the four years in New York had re-energized him. Although he didn't make any films during that time, he was able to spend more time watching films in the New York cinemas. He re-studied film masterpieces by maestros like Buster Keaton, Federico Fellini, Ozu Yasujiro and Robert Bresson. Those days enabled him to review and confirm his line of thinking about film.

After he returned to Korea in 2004, he immediately launched into his next project. He set up his own film production company, Production M, and produced his comeback film *Duelist. Duelist* displayeded LEE's characteristic splendid style, but was criticized for its simple storyline and self-conscious excess. This contributed to its failure at the box office. However, it was evaluated as a radical film that maximized the expression of cinematic language to the extreme, in a form of martial arts action as well as melodrama. Like his previous films, it produced a fanatical group of followers called *Duelist* 'addicts.' Although the film didn't gain a good response from the mainstream public, it gave the impression that LEE's cinematic world had become more solid.

LEE has completed his eighth film, *M*. Produced by CHO Sung-woo, who has worked with LEE since *Nowhere to Hide* as music director, *M* is about a best-selling novelist chasing the ghost of his first love. Under post-production at the time of this writing, *M* was to be introduced for the first time at the Toronto International Film Festival, which was held from September 6 to 15, 2007, and was released in Korea in October 2007.

Synopsis

Synopsis

Gagman (1988)

Working at a nightclub, LEE Jong-se (AHN Sung-ki) is a gagman who dreams of becoming a film director. However, due to his mental dysfunction, he is a helpless dreamer and unable to tell reality from a movie. He snoops around film sets wearing a moustache like Charlie Chaplin, the master of the silent era. He is also captivated by the grandiose idea of making a true film in a time with no masterpieces. In reality, he is just a stand-up gagman performing shows at third-class nightclubs, but Jong-se's ungrounded dream to surprise the world is encouraged by like-minded friends. One day LEE Jong-se goes to a barbershop and meets ne'er-do-well barber MOON Do-suk (BAE Chang-ho), who once had aspirations of becoming an actor. Watching MOON perform a part from an old action film, LEE tells him that he will cast him in the main role of his future film. Enthusiastically, Moon takes him at his word, sells his barbershop and undergoes eyelid surgery to become a serious actor. Meanwhile, OH Sun-young (HWANG Cine) happens to sit next to LEE Jong-se in a theater and pretends to be dating him in order to avoid some guys who are chasing her. Bored and indifferent to the world, this plucky girl follows him to his house after he tells her that he's a film director. While these three outsiders get to know each other, an armed runaway soldier (SON Chang-min) breaks into the club where Jong-se was performing stand-up comedy. Jong-se chats with the exhausted man, but the young runaway soldier suddenly commits suicide and his gun passes into Jong-se's hands. Finding himself unexpectedly in possession of a gun, Jong-se brings together Do-suk and Sun-young to take part in making a film. They consider themselves a legendary trio of robbers, but in reality they are just petty thieves robbing small clothing shops and supermarkets around the corner. With two lead characters and a gun for a prop, Jong-se tries to kick off his film about bank robbers and their getaway. So he makes an attempt to rob a small bank in a small town. With no fruitful results from the attempt, they appear on TV as a notorious criminal group at large. Whenever they attempt anything, Do-suk makes a silly mistake and they keep having to run away in their SUV and drive to a different town. One night the trio calls a car repairman (KIM Se-joon) to fix their car, which has broken down on the road, but when he recognizes them, he takes off running, and Do-suk accidentally shoots and kills him. Suddenly finding themselves a murderer and his accomplices, they run to Busan and try to ship themselves out, but become trapped on a train. Do-suk finally panics with regret and self-pity for giving up everything for a momentary dream, and tries to shoot Jong-se. At that moment, everything turns out to be a dream. Waking up from his daydream in Do-suk's barbershop, Jong-se still dreams about becoming a film director. After his dream goes up in smoke and he confronts the emptiness at the end of desire, LEE Jong-se and his companions begin dreaming of something else.

My Bride, My Love (1990)

One fine autumn day, Young-min (PARK Joong-hoon) is waiting on a park bench, preparing to propose to his beloved girlfriend and college classmate Mi-young (CHOI Jin-sil). They are 'old lovers' who have been dating for so long that they see each other as family. However, they haven't proceeded to the next step yet, and they expect to reach a different stage in their relationship. He tries to confess his love to her, but they start arguing over a misunderstanding instead. After some twists and turns, this quarreling couple finally arrives at a wedding ceremony with everyone's blessings. Believing that they truly love each other, this couple has a honeymoon that seems to be full of happiness. Mi-young decorates her husband's rice lunch with beans spelling 'I love you' and looks forward to seeing him come back from work. They nurture a sweet love, but not everything is smooth. On the first night of their marriage, Mi-young is afraid to become a married woman and she refuses to sleep with her husband. Despite loving him, she wants to be alone, and she shuts the door on him, leaving him in the hotel hallway. Like first love, the first kiss and the first marriage, everything looks new and awkward to Young-min and Mi-young. Their honeymoon becomes eventful with accidents. Mi-young hates it when Young-min brings a bunch of colleagues home without telling her in advance and Young-min becomes suspicious about the relationship between his wife and her former boss (SONG Young-chang) when they happen to meet him. Feeling vengeful, Young-min has a fling with his attractive boss (KIM Bo-yeon), and Mi-young regrets becoming a housewife stuck in the kitchen when she receives her ex-boyfriend's letter from overseas. Agonized with regret, she becomes possessed by old memories and leaves on a journey to escape from her daily routine. Their love and married life once seemed eternal, but now it falls into crisis. They experience many instances revealing that their belief that they are one is a misperception, as their routines and thoughts show differences. On the other hand, they are trying to find their own egos. Dreaming of becoming a writer, Young-min focuses on his writing. Meanwhile, Mi-young suffers an inferiority complex as he becomes more famous as a writer. One day, Mi-young suddenly contracts appendicitis and is carried to the hospital by ambulance. Even though her condition is not critical, Young-min feels guilty about his mistake and regrets what he has done. While he focuses on his writing at home, he suddenly feels lonely and runs to the hospital where Mi-young is hospitalized. Their relationship recovers as they reconcile with each other. As time passes, Young-min's dream finally comes true as his first novel is published. Enjoying his achievement, he recalls the memories of his youth, when he was feverishly in love. As a father, he has another chance to relive life with passion and a future with love. On Christmas day, as the world is covered with messages of blessing, he covers his son with a blanket while looking at his wife's picture.

First Love (1993)

Young-shin (KIM Hye-soo), a freshman at a regional art college, is a naive student with many dreams for the future. She has a kind father (CHOI Jong-won), a devoted mother (AN Hye-sook) and a cute sister (KIM Hye-Young) she can send to run secret errands to buy snacks at night. Although she is inexperienced and not knowledgeable about the world, she has rich feelings and a sense that leads her to expect something fantastic will happen in her college life. But big expectations bring big disappointment. Her college life doesn't bring any special events. One day, Young-shin sees a Chang-wook, a man from Seoul invited to direct her class in a play. About ten years older than Young-shin, Chang-wook is old-fashioned and a typical artist. He scratches his unwashed hair and speaks blunty while stepped in cigarette smoke and drinking. To a freshman with rosy dreams, Chang-wook looks like a high-brow man full of the self-consciousness of an artist. But who says a woman should be attracted to a bad man? Young-shin can't deny it, but she finds it strange to feel attracted to Chang-wook, who had given such a bad first impression. The truth about first love is that love has no reasons, and the things you look don't always follow reason and logic. Like a poet once said, love comes to you like a thief or a flash, and Young-shin falls into an unlikely love for Chang-wook, a love like the miracle of changing water into wine. Her whole world changes from the moment she falls in love. His every gesture becomes special, his words sound like music, and conversation with him becomes a poem. She writes a love letter filled with the racing of her heart, decorates her diary notes with heart marks and his name, and impulsively rides to his house on a bicycle to peep into his house over the fence. Young-shin can't control her foolish infatuation, and bursts out crying when she finally sees him after he failed to show up for their meeting. She is absorbed in love, and her daily life becomes full of dreams, fantasies and vain waiting. Perhaps knowing her mind, Chang-wook gives her a first kiss on a park bench under a flowering tree late at night. They begin meeting frequently; they go on a trip and spend a night together in a motel when Chang-wook gets drunk. They picture themselves in the future when they meet a happy old couple in a quiet temple. However, Chang-wook goes back to Seoul after finishing production on the play. He explains that his family has an important event. To see her beloved, Young-shin gets up her courage to buy a train ticket to go to Seoul for the first time in her life. After struggling to find his address, she finally arrives at his house. Standing motionless, Young-shin is forced to realize the secret of the world. Chang-wook, her first love, is a married man with a wife and child. After looking at the happy family gathering through a crack in the door, Young-shin turns away with a devastated heart, fighting back her tears. Her beautiful memory of first love ends abruptly.

The Affliction of Man (1994)

Everyday is a battle for manager AHN Sung-ki (AHN Sung-ki), who is in a new product development team at Osung Electronics. He is also the head of a family with concerns about his married brother's rent and his sister's marital woes. In addition, he is in danger at work for his incompetency. The stress torments him as his boss smothers him with criticism and a fresh generation of staff members arises, full of new suggestions. Whenever he comes to work after struggling in the hellish subway, his days start with rants from the boss and continue on to meetings and arguments with junior staff. In spite of his five years of experience, he hasn't come up with any brilliant ideas and his computer skills are still terrible. His junior employees are also suffering from the sorrows of the salaryman. Assistant manager CHOI Jong-won (CHOI Jong-won) likes attention and is a big talker at after-work dinners, but he is a 'never-promoted' assistant manager and is afraid of his nagging

wife at home. Director SONG Young-chang (SONG Young-chang) has a good academic background and high capabilities, but he is morbidly suspicious of his wife's fidelity, which keeps him busy monitoring his wife even during work hours. The helpless 'mama's boy' PARK Sang-min (PARK Sang-min), a newcomer, even asks his mother's permission when he wants to kiss a girl. Assistant manager CHO (CHO Sun-mook), in the advertising team, begins a dangerous affair with a young woman, and director YOON (YOON Joo-sang) takes pleasure in bullying his junior staff. None of them are respectable or right. Struggling to survive amid fierce competition, the poor salarymen have daily lives full of stress and agony. Their kids never see their father's faces and their authority in the family disappears as they feel the sorrows of breadwinning. They live in fear of losing their jobs, and they don't know when they will come down with a health problem from the stress, drinking and smoking in a society with the highest record of deaths among men in their forties. Their seven days pass with a sequence of anxiety, warlike commuting stress, stomachaches caused by the workplace pressure, stress over promotions and success, and suspicion about their wives. However, even though he is lost under the pressure of reality, manager AHN Sung-ki still treasures his dream of becoming an astronomer. He also has a dreamer's temperament, dancing to his favorite songs like 'My Dad's Youth' on rainy days, even though he is immersed in stress and fatigue. This film conveys the daily life and portraits of salarymen in Korea through daily episodes: the first day of newcomer PARK Sang-min (Monday), the company dinner (Tuesday), overtime work (Wednesday), Director YOON's explosion and the releasing of stress through karaoke (Thursday), and the firing of Director YOON and Manager AHN's fleeing from work (Friday).

Their Last Love Affair (1996)

Professor and poet Young-min (KIM Gab-soo) treats journalist Young-hee (KANG Soo-yeon) to dinner to thank her for writing a review of his poem. Although he has a wife and two kids, Young-min falls for Young-hee at first sight. He secretly asks her out through his fellow professor (KIM Hak-chul) and Young-hee also feels some inevitable connection with him. Their love begins with feverish infatuation. In their love, no sense of morality or guilt matters to them. Young-min is eager to meet his lover, cheating on his devoted wife. He tries to spend more time with Young-hee, making the excuse that he is working. However, their semi-relationship is more stressful to Young-hee, who is single. Hating the reality of having to going back to their own and hide their relationship, Young-hee suffers a feeling of deficiency because of the love she wants to show to people. She is tiring of the discreet dates and the motels. Eventually Young-min finds a place to spend time with her. He finds a humble room near a quiet beach. From then, they live like an unmarried couple who haven't bothered to register yet. Their love doesn't demand any concerns about image or self-esteem. They suddenly start kissing each other while eating greasy chicken meat, or start making love while having meals, even getting their knees grazed from rolling with each other on the floor naked. It's a form of blind love. They feel happy about staying in a place where they can wake up and have coffee together naked. But living together is another reality. They fight each other over washing dishes or watching a TV program. The truth of 'intense love' is a fierce conflict, a fight, morbid obsession and blinded preoccupation. The woman lets the man down by saying, 'You have to go back home,' and he becomes angry and jealous when told she has a blind date set up by a matchmaker. In this way, their situation already shows signs of a break-up. Love is past its expiration date and they have places to return to. Even though they had a relevant relationship, love doesn't last forever. Young-min and Young-hee turn their backs on each other and return to their separate lives.

Nowhere to Hide (1999)

Detectives in a homicide team in the police force are not so different from the brutal villains who they have to catch and arrest. Hot-blooded Detective WOO Young-gu (PARK Joong-hoon) is notorious for his explosive temper even within the tough homicide team of the Western District police station. He is a tenacious and passionate pursuer who never gives up until he has caught his prey, strongly believing that a 'detective's job is only about catching.' Hot-tempered fighter WOO is busy as usual brushing off the group of gangsters attacking him. One day a murder occurs in their district. The victim (SONG Young-chang), a drug trafficker, is found on some unfrequented steps, brutally slaughtered on a rainy day. The police can't find any clues due to the bad weather. The homicide team, including Detective WOO, is put on this murder case, and they begin their stakeout. It is their main job to wait for their ambush. During their operation, Detectives WOO and KIM (Jang Dong-gun) at times imagine having hot meat soup to forget their tiring day. After a long wait, the two detectives arrest Zzang-gu (PARK Sang-myun) and Young-bae (AHN Jae-mo), as accomplices to the murder, and find out about the main suspect. The culprit turns out to be JANG Sung-min (AHN Sung-ki), who is notorious as a cold-blooded, manipulative and protean criminal. Fifteen days after the murder, the detectives sneak into the house of KIM Joo-yeon (CHOI Ji-woo), the culprit's girlfriend, to confront JANG, but they eventually lose him in the maze-like back streets after a chaotic fight. JANG calmly disappears from the police dragnet in another episode. Detective KIM accidentally kills someone with a clue about JANG while he is chasing him, and Detective WOO tries to comfort him. 42 days after the murder, the detectives hear from a source that JANG is planning a deal on a running train, and they disguise themselves to catch him there. After a fierce fight, they fail to arrest him again, and detective KIM is stabbed. Filled with anger, Detective WOO and other detectives go down to JANG's hometown, expecting him to appear at his mother's funeral. The culprit finally turns up, and Detective WOO and JANG confront each other in a final duel at some deserted ruins under a downpour of rain. The final duel between the pursuer and the pursued, the detective and thecriminal, is destiny.

Duelist (2005)

18th century Korea. The film begins with voluble blacksmith Bong-chul (Yoon Joo-sang) babbling his stories to people around him. He is rattling on about a voluptuous lady (KIM Bo-yeon) he met one night, but suddenly the film moves to

another story about a crowded marketplace. In the marketplace, counterfeit money is being circulated chaotically. Jwapo District Office's *Pogyo* detective Nam-soon (HA Ji-won) is a hothead, unlike other women in that she can't control her temper and she leads with her fists. Nam-soon's partner is the considerate and experienced *Pogyo* AN. Her polar opposite, he is more meticulous when he approaches cases; they counterbalance each other. In order to find the source of the counterfeit money and the criminal distributor, Nam-soon and AN are investigating the marketplace. One day, feeling more suspicious about someone than usual, Nam-soon starts chasing a man in a mask. She chases him through backstreets and gaps between fences, but the elusive man disappears, leaving the two detectives far behind. All the detectives gathered in the Jwapo office are busy talking about the source of the counterfeit money, and Nam-soon soon convinces herself that the suspect in the mask is the figure with the key to the case. After some searching and investigating, Nam-soon discovers that the suspect is working for *Byungpan* (SONG Young-chang), a man with enormous power. She discovers the suspect's nickname is Sad Eyes (GANG Dong-won). To catch a tiger, you have to step into the tiger's den. Nam-soon disguises herself as a *gisaeng* and slips into *Byungpan*'s house, but Sad Eyes senses who she is the moment he sees her. The more they encounter each other, the more Nam-soon has to fight herself away from falling for the attractive Sad Eyes rather than seeing him as a criminal. Sad Eyes also has had feelings for her from the first moment he faced her in the marketplace. Oblivious to their duties, both will fall in love with one another. As *Byungpan Daegam* discovers that the police's investigation is closing in on him, he orders Sad Eyes to kill the Jwapo Jongsa officer (DO Young-gu) on a snowy day. In the meantime, Sad Eyes hands Nam-soon a critical clue against *Byungpan*, his surrogate father to whom he is devote. Convinced that Byung-pan is a criminal, the Jwapo detectives join forces with an enforcement squad and suddenly raid his house on his daughter's wedding day. Surrounded by police, *Byungpan* meets his end, while Nam-soon and Sad Eyes confront each other for a last duel (or romance) in the transparent darkness.

M (2007)

The attractive author of bestselling novels, HAN Min-woo (GANG Dong-won) one day feels a strange gaze fall on the back of his head. He is used to others looking at him all the time, but he can't stop thinking about strange things. It's like someone is watching him. He can't explain whether this situation is happening in a dream or reality. His chief editor keeps urging him to make commercial stories, and his future father-in-law (SONG Young-chang) is a materialistic snob. Those people around him are not so different from his occasional nightmares. Restless and distracted, he is in a slump and unable to write a word. One night, on his way home after a regular meeting with the chief editor in an odd bar called 'Lupin,' he meets a woman in a purple dress. Min-woo tells her stories about his new book and she sings a sweet song for him. It all disappears when he is woken up by a phone call from his fiancée Eun-hye (GONG Hyo-jin). She says 'I love you' and he

tells her he loves her too, but Min-woo's mind is preoccupied with the girl he met at the Lupin. He tries to call her number, but he only hears a message that the number is out of service. He can't get out of his mind the image of a woman in a purple dress, and in his fantasy he associates her image with his first love and muse, Mi-mi (LEE Yeon-hee). He recalls his memory of first love with Mi-mi and finally starts writing. Popular high school student Min-woo visits her family's hair shop, and Mi-mi's heart is bursting with joy. The girl runs toward him and hops on his bicycle instead of saying 'Don't leave.' The bicycle rides along the beach, and their moment in the sunset fades into a memory of first love. His old friends tell him her story. Although Min-woo wanders about in search of the haunting memory of his first love, the Umbrella Man, another man in pursuit of her, tries to tear them apart. Can these two desperate lovers escape from this unwanted intruder?

Filmography

Filmography

Gagman (*Gaegeumaen*)

1988 / 127 min / 35mm / 1.85:1

Production Company: Taeheung Production Company

Screenplay: LEE Myung-Se

Cinematography: YOO Young-gil

Editing: KIM Hyun

Music: KIM Soo-chul

Lighting: CHA Jung-nam

Starring: AHN Sung-ki, BAE Chang-ho, HWANG Cine, JEON Moo-song, JO Joo-mi

International Sales: Taeheung Production Company

My Bride My Love (*Naeui sarang naeui shinbu*)

1990 / 111 min / 35mm / 1.85:1
Production Company: Samho Film Inc.
Screenplay: LEE Myung-Se
Cinematography: YOO Young-gil
Editing: KIM Hyun
Music: JEONG Sung-jo
Lighting: KIM Dong-ho
Starring: PARK Joong-hoon, CHOE Jin-shil, KIM Bo-yeon, JEON Moo-song, SONG Young-chang
International Sales: Production M

First Love (*Cheot sarang*)

1993 / 108 min / 35mm / 1.85:1
Production Company: Samho Film Inc.
Screenplay: LEE Myung-Se
Cinematography: YOO Young-gil
Editing: KIM Hyun
Music: SONG Byeong-joon
Lighting: KIM Dong-ho
Starring: SONG Young-chang, KIM Hye-soo, JO Min-gi, CHOE Jong-won, AN Hye-sook
International Sales: Production M

Affliction of Man (*Namjaneun goereowo*)

1994 / 110 min / 35mm / 1.85:1
Production Company: Ik-young Film
Screenplay: LEE Myung-Se
Cinematography: YOO Young-gil
Editing: KIM Hyun
Music: CHOE Joon-sung
Lighting: KIM Dong-ho
Starring: AHN Sung-ki, PARK Sang-min, KIM Hye-soo, SONG Young-chang, YOON Joo-sang, CHOE Jong-won
International Sales: Production M

Their Last Love Affair (*Jidokhan sarang*)

1996 / 106 min / 35mm / 1.85:1
Production Company: CINE2000
Screenplay: LEE Myung-Se
Cinematography: JUNG Gwang-seok
Editing: KIM Hyun
Music: SONG Byung-joon
Lighting: SHIN Hak-seong
Starring: GANG Soo-yeon, KIM Gab-soo, KIM Hak-cheol, LEE Hwa-young, JO Joo-mi
International Sales: CINE2000

Nowhere to Hide (*Injeong sajeong bol geot eopda*)

1999 / 112 min / 35mm / 1.85:1

Production Company: Taewon Entertainment Inc.

Screenplay: LEE Myung-Se

Cinematography: JUNG Gwang-seok, SONG Hang-ki

Editing: GO Im-pyo

Music: Jo Seong-woo, KIM Dae-hong

Lighting: KIM Il-joon

Starring: PARK Joong-hoon, AHN Sung-ki, JANG Dong-kun, CHOE Ji-woo, SONG Young-chang

International Sales: CJ Entertainment

Duelist (*Hyungsa*)

2005 / 113 min / 35mm / 10170ft / 2.35:1 / Color / Dolby Digital

Production Company: Production M Inc.

Executive Producer: KIM Jae-young

Producers: LEE Myung-Se, Oh Eun-shil, O Sumi

Screenplay: LEE Myung-Se, LEE Hae-kyung

Original Story: BANG Hak-ki

Cinematography: Ki S. HWANG

Editing: Go Im-pyo

Music: CHO Sung-woo

Lighting: SHIN Kyeong-man

Recording: LEE Sang-wook

Sound: PARK Jun-O

Art Director: LEE Hyeong-joo, CHO Keun-hyun

Costumes: CHONG Kyong-hee

Make-up: HWANG Hyun-kyu

Starring: HA Ji-won, GANG Dong-won, AHN Sung-ki

International Sales: Production M

M

2007 / 109 min / 35mm, 2.35:1

Production Company: Production M Inc.

Screenplay: LEE Myung-Se

Cinematography: HONG Gyung-pyo

Editing: GO Im-pyo

Music: JO Sung-woo

Lighting: CHOE Chul-soo

Starring: GANG Dong-won, LEE Yeon-hee, GONG Hyo-jin

International Sales: Showbox/Mediaplex Inc.

About the Author

JANG Byung-won

JANG Byung-won was born in Seoul in 1972. He graduated from the Department of Korean Language Education at Dongguk University. He received a master's degree in film theory from Chung-Ang University. He is a Ph.D. student in film theory at Chung-Ang University's Film Art Department. He is currently the editor-in-chief of film weekly magazine *FILM 2.0*.

Index

Affliction of Man, 23, 24, 46, 59, 91, 100, 101, 105, 111, 140, 150, 163
AHN Sung-ki, 22, 24, 43, 46, 59, 82, 108, 110, 145, 150, 151, 154, 161, 163, 164, 165
André Bazin, 71, 133

BAE Chang-ho, 30, 79, 82, 85, 140, 146, 161
Billy Wilder, 104, 109, 113, 120
Buster Keaton, 28, 29, 115, 116, 141

Charlie Chaplin, 28, 82, 145

Dazai Osamu, 83, 125
Duelist, 9, 22, 31, 33, 51, 52, 53, 54, 55, 58, 59, 61, 63, 64, 67, 68, 70, 71, 88, 91, 104, 110, 114, 117, 118, 122, 123, 125, 131, 142, 154, 164

Edgar Allan Poe, 124
Ernst Lubitsch, 104, 109

First Love, 21, 22, 23, 24, 25, 31, 37, 41, 43, 46, 48, 49, 54, 57, 59, 64, 65, 67, 68, 70, 71, 75, 77, 87, 91, 94, 95, 96, 99, 100, 105, 107, 108, 126, 127, 128, 129, 140, 149, 162
fundamentalist, 10, 18, 29, 30, 69

Gagman, 12, 13, 17, 19, 20, 30, 41, 42, 43, 45, 46, 56, 63, 64, 70, 79, 82, 83, 84, 85, 86, 87, 88, 91, 100, 128, 138, 140, 145, 161
GANG Dong-won 33, 52, 120, 156, 165

HA Ji-won, 33, 52, 110, 155, 165
Hollywood, 10, 20, 27, 32, 42, 43, 54, 60, 63, 68, 69, 104, 141
HWANG Cine, 146, 161

IM Kwon-taek, 18, 23
integrated film, 17, 18, 31, 33, 40, 70, 71

KANG Soo-yeon, 25, 106, 113, 152
KANG Woo-suk, 21
KIM Hye-soo, 23, 65, 87, 149, 162, 163
KIM Tae-kyun, 21, 86
Korean New Wave, 11, 12, 80

LEE Jang-ho, 79

M, 13, 38, 44, 45, 47, 48, 49, 51, 53, 54, 55, 56, 58, 59, 61, 63, 64, 65, 67, 68, 69, 70, 71, 89, 91, 93, 99, 105, 118, 122, 123, 124, 125, 126, 127, 128, 131, 132, 142, 156
MacGuffin, 31, 38, 56, 57, 58, 61
My Bride, My Love, 20, 22, 38, 41, 48, 49, 50, 57, 59, 67, 68, 70, 77, 80, 83, 86, 88, 91, 92, 93, 95, 97, 100, 140, 147
Myriam, 123, 124, 125
MYUNG Kae-nam, 26

Nowhere to Hide, 9, 22, 26, 30, 41, 51, 52, 53, 55, 57,

58, 59, 63, 64, 68, 69, 70, 71, 82, 86, 88, 91, 97, 104, 107, 108, 110, 111, 112, 113, 114, 117, 118, 123, 141, 142, 153, 164

Ozu Yasujiro, 28, 30, 116, 141

PARK, Joong-hoon 26, 38, 108, 109, 110, 112, 113, 147, 153, 162, 164
PARK Pyoung-sik, 139

realism, 10, 11, 12, 42, 43, 44, 47, 70, 72, 80, 106, 107
Richard Corliss, 25

Seoul Art College, 139, 140

Their Last Love Affair, 23, 24, 25, 51, 57, 68, 88, 99, 104, 105, 106, 107, 113, 123, 140, 152, 163

YOO Young-gil, 85, 161, 162, 163